C. R. Hensman

Sun Yat-sen

SCM PRESS LTD

334 01553 7

First published 1971
by SCM Press Ltd
56 Bloomsbury Street London

© *SCM Press Ltd 1971*

Printed in Great Britain by
Billing & Sons Limited
Guildford and London

scm centrebooks · six christians

---

already published
Martin Luther King / *Kenneth Slack*
Simone Weil / *David Anderson*
Karl Barth / *John Bowden*
Teilhard de Chardin / *Vernon Sproxton*
Sun Yat-sen / *C. R. Hensman*

in preparation
George Bell / *Kenneth Slack*

Contents

Contents

1 Introduction

Sun Yat-sen died of cancer in Peking in 1925. Even to those of us whose years of active work are past that must seem a long time ago. The world seems to have changed several times since the 1920s. China has changed almost beyond recognition, and so has much of the rest of Asia. The days of the greatness of more recent Asian leaders like Gandhi and Nehru seem remote, as we try to grapple with the political, moral and cultural problems of living properly in the 1970s. Even Nasser and Guevara are becoming only memories. It is no wonder that Woodrow Wilson and Lloyd George, who were contemporaries of Sun, belong to an age which is long past. Sun Yat-sen should, perhaps, be rightly placed with them, rather than with people who still have a meaning for the world in which the most sensitive people are agonizing about what can be done about a South East Asia engaged in a people's war against the might of the United States, about the challenge of the Naxalites in India and about the Arab–Israeli conflict in the Middle East.

Yet, let us consider this. The people who dominate the political scene in the world's most populous nation were at one time chosen colleagues of Sun Yat-sen, and the work that Mao Tse-tung and Chou En-lai have been doing since his death has been a continuation of tasks he began, and on which he worked together with them. The peasants and workers whose creative labours have transformed China are very much at the centre of our attention these days, if we are at all alert to what is happening around us; and the creation of the conditions in which they could begin *their* economic and political tasks was one of the main aims of Sun. A political figure whose activities are still of worldwide significance, Generalissimo Chiang Kai-shek, was also a close colleague of Sun; it was Sun who first helped to advance him to prominence and power. Sun's widow, Soong Chingling, whose own work entitles her to be called one of the distinguished statesmen of our age, carried on his work, and continued to do so until the 1960s. It is not routine work we are thinking of, or men and women who merely hold or have held office. It is work, and persons, whose impact on China and the world still eludes the understanding of most of us.

The personal links are to some extent due to the accident of longevity. Chairman Mao and Premier Chou of China are in their seventies. If Sun's work is still with us in our day it will have to be shown how that is possible, when so much has changed. The men and women whose words and work live on after their generation has passed away are the very great. There are very few of them in history. There are very few indeed in our century. We are advancing very high claims for Sun in considering him as a figure of importance for our day.

The role played by Sun Yat-sen in the history which was made in his own lifetime has yet to receive the attention it deserves. Sun's development as a man and as a statesman was deeply involved with the specific details of Chinese history and international politics. It is necessary for us to pay more attention to the historical context and to political issues than to biographical details, which are in any case rather scarce, as Sun was not a man to draw attention to his private life. Students of Chinese affairs are so badly served by the scholars and journalists who 'specialize' on China that there are more than the usual difficulties to be overcome in discussing the life and work of one of the leaders of the Chinese Revolution. Even before Sun became socialist and anti-imperialist in his policies there were campaigns conducted by westerners to discredit his work, and belittle his importance. For Sun's success in organizing the overthrow of Manchu rule could lead to further successes in removing the causes of the poverty and backwardness of the Chinese people. Sun was one of the first Third World leaders to get the kind of treatment in western newspapers and books which, unfortunately, is reserved for people who threaten western interests and notions of what is good for Asians and Africans.

A good example of some of the more sober attempts at denigration appeared soon after the 1911 Revolution, in a book called *Recent Events and Present Policies in China*, by J. O. P. Bland:

> Of Sun's sincerity, of his courage, modesty, patriotism and intelligence, there can be no question. His remarkable personality and romantic career have rightly won for him the admiration and devotion of many of his countrymen and his influence with the younger generation of foreign-educated Cantonese is undeniable. Nevertheless, when all is said and done, he remains a dreamer of dreams; his ideals of government and reform are the result of undigested socialistic theories combined with a purely imaginative and idealised conception of China and the Chinese.
>
> A semi-Oriental, reared and trained amongst Europeans, he reveals the Oriental's peculiar lack of historical consciousness, unredeemed by the European's attitude of scientific inquiry; and his writings, as well as his public performances, display the almost inhuman lack of humour which characterises many of the world's political crusaders. His attitude and utterances in regard to the Manchus are in themselves quite sufficient to prove Sun Yat-sen a blind leader of the blind; in the cold light of history, they appear so fantastic and childish that, were it not for their visible effect upon Young China and Old England, they would scarcely be deserving of attention. . . .[1]

The power of people with opinions like these, and more extreme ones, to determine their fate has been one of the obstacles to independence and progress which the Chinese people have succeeded in removing. It is not the purpose of this book, and it is not within my competence, to provide a history of the early stages of the Chinese revolutionary struggle to make up for the misinformation and misrepresentation of the record. Sun is in no danger of being forgotten by the people who matter, and his fame is likely to grow among those, in China and outside, who are making the world of the twenty-first century. The Chinese themselves have lived too close to the history, and struggled too much over the political issues, not to know what Sun's achievements were worth. When they achieved what they saw as their liberation, in 1949, they paid tribute to Sun Yat-sen. In the historic words of the leader under whom Sun's revolutionary work was developed and continued, he was 'the great pioneer of China's Revolution'. In 1966 the centenary of his birth was celebrated in China. It was Sun's fellow countrymen who gave him his honoured place by following his lead, supporting him, protecting his life and fighting alongside him, and it is their children and grand-children who acknowledge his greatness.

We are not being presumptuous, therefore, in selecting this particular Chinese – no 'semi-Oriental' – to write about, and in reproducing some of the documents and speeches which indicate the programmes and policies for which Sun fought and laboured. Today some of us are better able than we were to understand the Third World, the revolutionary Third World, in the creation of which Sun was one of the pioneering figures. It is easier to acknowledge – even if we may do so with regret – that in a good part of the world the finest and most sensitive men and women take very seriously the tasks of a political and economic revolution and of the struggle against the imperialism which benefits some in Europe and North America. Sun had friends in the West who admired and supported him, but none of them could in their time have appreciated the nature of his aims and the quality of his achievements. Even today people are so brainwashed with imperialist and racist ideas and passions that some must find it difficult to admire Sun for his role in aiding the struggle of the Filipino revolutionaries.

To write of Sun as a Christian is another matter. Bernard

10

Martin, in his interesting biography, reports that Sun once remarked: 'I do not belong to the Christianity of the churches but to the Christianity of Jesus, who was a revolutionary.' Another remark he made was: 'I am a messenger of God to help men to obtain equality and freedom.' As Sun was dying, Bernard Martin writes, he told his brother-in-law, T. V. Soong: 'You are a Christian; I, too, am a Christian.'[2]

Sun clearly thought it important that he should identify himself as a Christian, though, as we shall see, he had nothing to gain materially or politically by doing so. He was not the kind of 'Christian' of whom those in control of church establishments – especially church establishments in colonial and semi-colonial lands – have been proud. Let us anticipate the story of Sun's life, and set down the record: he was a life-long organizer of armed revolution; he fought with all the means he could command against western (including missionary) power and interests in East Asia; he admired Lenin and was highly thought of by Lenin, and he welcomed the Bolshevik Revolution; he put communists in key positions in his government, and indeed, by the definitions of our own day, he was himself a 'communist'; he divorced his first wife in order to marry Soong Ching-ling.

Why then, it may be wondered, should one write of Sun as though he had been a great Christian? The question is – it is meant to be – provocative. Christians have never been backward in sedulously flattering men in high office who are church members or are favourably inclined to church members or church interests. Curiously enough, when we come to the Christian who became the first President of the Chinese Republic and, later, head of the Canton revolutionary government, the story is different. Sun was the hero of a nation of, at that time, four hundred million people. But he never was a model which Asian or African Christians were encouraged to follow. Missionaries were actually working against Sun, and some were actively

11

engaged, soon after the 1911 Revolution, in working for Yuan Shih-kai, the militarist and counter-revolutionary. Sun attained rank and prestige which no other Asian Christian has approached, at least in modern times. Yet, unlike Syngman Rhee of Korea and Chiang Kai-shek and Ngo Dinh Diem, he was considered a 'bad' Christian. He was not loyal.

If Sun appears as the subject of one of a series of books on Christians, it is not because it is intended to suggest that he deserves to be rehabilitated by the church establishments, and belatedly claimed for what he was – politically the most important Christian in the non-European world in modern times. Rather it is to honour Sun for daring to be the model of a 'bad' Christian. Only those who know the problems that Asian Christians have had over their political identity and loyalties can fully appreciate the significance of discussing Sun in these terms. One remembers how shocked and outraged the church establishments were when, in the later 1940s, they discovered that many Chinese Christians had been and were for the Chinese Revolution. The easy assumption that Christians cannot *as Christians* feel committed to join in the cultural revolution or the popular wars of national liberation under the leadership of 'communists' makes a discussion of Sun's life and work of more than sectarian interest. That is, a discussion of this kind must help to explain to those who have no way of assessing theologically the reactionary and counter-revolutionary influence of church establishments that Sun was a good Christian.

To lead the poor and oppressed to rebel against their oppressors, and to join in the work of ridding the world of the violence, injustice and economic backwardness which causes impoverishment and oppression – these, one would suppose, are revolutionary tasks which Christians can ignore only by making their faith in Jesus Christ meaningless. Sun Yat-sen's commitment as a Christian is a lesson not merely for Christians in the Third World but, as any discussion of his work must make clear, for all Christians.

NOTES

1. J. O. P. Bland, *Recent Events and Present Policies in China*, Heinemann 1912, pp. 51–2.
2. Bernard Martin, *Strange Vigour*, Heinemann 1944, p. 226.

2 A Young Peasant Rebels

Kwangtung, the southernmost coastal province of China, has the same area as Great Britain. At the mouth of the Si Kiang, or Pearl River, which flows through it into the sea, is the city of Kwangchow, or Canton. This, the major city of south China, is 1,200 miles from Peking, the capital of China. A hundred years ago the people of Kwangtung had got to know, better than those of any other province, the ways of the armed foreigners from the distant lands. These were, they knew, foreigners who had no respect for their laws or well-being, and men who freely used their weapons. The people of Kwangtung had strong feelings of hostility towards the foreigners, who had several times attacked them and who had also taken possession of part of their province. The ineffectiveness of the imperial rulers only increased the contempt these southern people felt for the Manchu court.

The village of Choyhung was about forty miles away from Canton. Sun Tao-chuan and his wife would, like their neighbours in Choyhung, have lived in complete obscurity but for the fact that in 1866, probably on 12 November, they had a second child, a son, who was to become the most famous of Kwangtung's many famous sons. The boy, fifteen years younger than the first son, was named Tai-cheong. He was later to be known by other names, among them Sun Wen and Sun Yat-sen.

Tao-chuan cultivated about three acres of rented land. This meant that life was hard, since the land was not very productive; rent had to be paid, taxes had to be paid, and on what was left Tao-chuan and his wife, the widowed wives of his two brothers, and three children had to be fed and clothed. China had no caste system, and labour in the fields was neither undignified nor demeaning. Peasants traditionally enjoyed a higher social status than merchants, and it was soldiering that was looked down upon, with good reason. Peasants were the main producers of wealth, and peasant boys who showed unusual aptitude for learning could rise to high office in the state as officials. But for some time now the life of the peasants of China had been very far from the ideal. The citizens of the great Chinese Empire – the oldest and grandest in the world – had a hard time keeping themselves alive. Tao-chuan's two brothers had both died abroad, seeking their fortunes as coolies.

The Chinese peasants were among the most diligent and efficient workers in the world, but hard work alone does not produce results. For agriculture there is needed continual investment of effort and money in new irrigation works, in enrichment of the soil, in the bringing of fresh land into cultivation to meet the production and consumption needs of a growing population, and in the improvement of skills. Neglect of these responsibilities by the government had forced the proletarianized Chinese agricultural labourers to migrate in search of better opportunities. In the areas of the world where rapid economic expansion was then taking place – the British and Dutch colonies in South East Asia, the west coast of North America and in plantations all over the world – there was a growing demand for cheap and highly efficient labour. By their thrift some of these labourers had been able to find a better life as traders and the owners of small businesses which did not compete with the big commercial capitalist enterprises. Sun's brother, Te-chang, when still a boy left for Hawaii and made good there. Te-chang returned home on a visit when his younger brother was eleven, and it was clear to Tao-chuan that his elder son had prospered. Though the loss of a labourer in the fields would add to the peasant's difficulties, the younger boy was sent, in his thirteenth year, to join his brother in Hawaii.

'I am a coolie, the son of a coolie. I was born with the poor and am still poor,' Sun Yat-sen is reported to have said at the end of his life.

His widow wrote in 1927:

> Sun Yat-sen came from the people. He told me a great deal about his early days. He came from the peasantry. Sun was poor. Not until he was fifteen years old did he have shoes for his feet, and he lived in a hilly region where it is not easy to be a barefoot boy. His family, until he and his brother were grown, lived almost from hand to mouth, in a hut. As a child he ate the cheapest food – not rice, for rice was too dear. His main nourishment was sweet potatoes.
>
> Many times has Sun told me that it was in those early days, as the poor son of a poor peasant family, that he became a revolutionary. He was determined that the lot of the Chinese peasant should not continue to be so wretched, that little boys in China should have shoes to wear and rice to eat. . . .

Soong Ching-ling's words were written in desperation, at a time of national crisis, and the element of romantic exaggeration may be pardoned. But there is no possible doubt that the childhood experiences of those first twelve years in Choyhung came to be very important in Sun's life. The fact of the great poverty of the Chinese people, the whys and wherefores of it, and the desire to change it, had begun to occur to an unusually sensitive boy. In Kwangtung people were not accepting their personal poverty as unavoidable. It was possible to improve their lot, and the lot of their families, by leaving the domains of the Chinese Emperor and his corrupt and inefficient officials. It was not possible to do so by staying at home. Why was this so? Why were the officials allowed to be corrupt? Why had so much to be paid in taxes and rent? The officials failed to keep the villages secure against the pirates who infested the area, thus adding to the hardships and miseries of the cultivators and their families. The people who stayed behind submitted to all this; and they indulged in a lot of superstititious practices.

It is in the nature of children to ask questions, even if they

16

are put off by the meaningless or confused answers that grown-ups give. Sun recalled in later life how he was pained by the cruelty inflicted on his younger sister when the agony of foot-binding was imposed on her, and how he asked if it was necessary. When his other duties permitted, he attended the local school, where he found the senseless ritual of rote-learning very irksome. He dared to ask, as hundreds of children are bold enough to do all over the world, why he should learn something without knowing what it meant. The punishment he got told him something about the system, and when he grew older he was able to see how the Manchu tyranny was maintained by the prevention of genuine learning and critical thinking.

After his departure for Hawaii in 1879 Sun was never to spend a long period in Choyhung. He had all the benefits of a boyhood grounded in village life in China without the drawbacks. His mind had been stimulated by gossip about the adventures of emigrants, by the irreverent talk which must have been heard in a rebelliously-inclined province like Kwangtung, and by the ferment of the times. On that education he was to build in later years. But before he was forced to conform and become just another poor, over-worked and superstitious peasant, he emigrated. And in the years of schooling in Hawaii he had time and leisure to read and reflect, and get the broader perspective of world history and worldwide developments in which to place his own past and future life. The kind of school to which he went was designed to produce people who conformed to another type of society. Sun was one of those few who escape being imprisoned by schools and universities. Thanks to his brother's generosity, he did not have to work as a labourer; before his admission to school, he worked in the shop which Te-chang had managed to buy.

In 1883, in his seventeenth year, Sun returned to Choyhung. It is likely that his decision to become a Christian led to the family decision that he should return. The fact is that

17

the young schoolboy had come to have a mind of his own, partly as a consequence of being away from his home.

Village China was for over a thousand years the essential China. Life in the village cannot be described as 'rural idiocy' and Chinese villagers were not 'oafs'. Comparisons with country life in feudal or industrialized Europe would be misleading. Any attempt to eliminate the causes of the poverty and misery of the Chinese people could only have been made by the peasants. To Sun and a friend of his who had returned to Choyhung after going to school in Shanghai, the fatalism and superstition of their elders must have seemed the chief obstacle to any change for the better. What could they do? China had been a great country in the past, and it would not be great again unless the people were stirred into revolt. Sun and his boyhood playmates had heard a good deal about the great Taiping Rebellion. One of Sun's uncles had actually fought in the Taiping armies, and in the games the boys played it is said that Sun played the role of Hung Hsiu-chuan, the Taiping leader, a native of Kwangtung. The fresh memory of a major rebellion by the peasants against the Ching dynasty was part of the living culture of village life in Kwangtung.

The Taiping kingdom had been brought to an end only two years before Sun was born. It had begun in 1850, and Hung Hsiu-chuan had worked out an ideology which had many elements of Christian belief and practice. The rebels had defeated a succession of imperial armies sent against them, and established their rule throughout a vast area of China, including parts of Kwangtung. Their capital had been set up in Nanking in 1853. Millions of peasants and others, who wanted to join in overthrowing the oppressive and unpopular imperial government, had followed Hung, and at one time the Taipings had come close to winning power in north China, too. Their policies had included redistribution of land and the equality of men and women. But dissensions among the leaders and their increasingly autocratic style of rule alienated their supporters, and weakened the Taipings. The imperial armies and navies were reorganized, but it was after many years and because of modern weapons and leadership by the foreign imperial powers that the Manchus succeeded in overthrowing the rule of the Taipings. (The British General Charles Gordon took a leading part in the final campaigns.) The followers of the Taipings were slaughtered by the millions. Over ten millions, possibly twice or three times that number, were killed. However, as the Chinese historian Li Chien-Hung notes:

> The innovations which the Taipings attempted to introduce into their political programme, such as the equal distribution of land, the plan to build steamships, railways, factories, and modern industries, the demand for equality between nation and nation, as well as between man and man, and even the simplification of the Chinese language, created an indelible impression in Chinese memories.[1]

It must also be added that the people could not easily have forgotten the fact that they had taken up arms against their rulers, beaten their armies, and actually established their own government. The western-supported attempt to crush the Taipings did not succeed in getting rid of all those who had taken part in the rebellion. Too many Chinese had been involved.

To the boys who played and talked together in the villages of Kwangtung in the 1870s and 1880s this, the greatest of all rebellions, would have been far from a memory. The discontents which had given rise to the rebellion, and to various other major uprisings of the period, must have been felt even more keenly than before. The British and French, who had helped to prop up the decaying Manchu-ruled order against the Taipings, had themselves committed aggression against it from 1858 to 1860, and had occupied Canton. There was no lack of reminders that the existing government was incapable of preventing Chinese from being attacked and humiliated in their own country and throughout the world.

The boy Sun had himself seen how Chinese were subject to racial insult even in Hawaii. He had returned to Choyhung to live the life of a peasant, participating in the superstitious ritual of village religion. He rebelled against such a life. He openly criticized the submission of the Chinese people to the rule of a small minority, and he pointed out the futility of petitioning against corruption through a bureaucracy which was itself steeped in corruption. Then he challenged the village itself by desecrating one of the sacred shrines. The village elders responded to this by getting Taochuan to send his son away.

Hong Kong, a part of Kwangtung but not under Manchu rule, was a much freer place than Choyhung. The young rebel resumed his studies. In close and continuous touch with his country, but also away from it in some ways, he was able to look at what was happening and to find other Chinese who shared his views. Though Hong Kong was a British colony, Sun lived among the Chinese who formed the overwhelming majority of its inhabitants. Sun was already there when war broke out between China and France. The French had been moving into Annam for some time, and the Chinese government, which had an obligation to protect the Vietnamese, had tried to avoid war with France. Eventually the French captured some Chinese camps on the Chinese border itself, and there was a short war (1884–5) in which the French got what they wanted, even though the Chinese armies had not been defeated. For Sun this fresh demonstration of how under the Manchus China could be treated with contempt was a new lesson in practical politics: 'From 1885, i.e. from the time of our defeat in the war with France, I set myself the object of the overthrow of the Ching Dynasty and the establishment of a Chinese Republic in its ruins.'[2]

His first idea was to join a military academy – an understandable response to the situation. But no suitable one existed. (Years later, another Chinese who was to become famous, Lin Piao, found that there was a military academy, founded by Sun, which people wanting to fight for the revolution could join.) Sun decided in the end to join the new medical college in Hong Kong. He started his five-year course in 1887, passing in 1892 as the first graduate of the college. He then went to practise his profession in the Portuguese-ruled territory of Macao. His work as a surgeon there was stopped when the Portuguese used some old regulation to deny those without Portuguese diplomas the right to practise. Sun had to leave his post.

The years in medical college provided something more important than a scientific and clinical training. The process by which the young peasant developed into the revolutionary was continued during those years.

> For four years I gave up all my time free from studies to the cause of revolutionary propaganda, travelling backward and forward between Hong Kong and Amoy. At that time I had scarcely any supporters, with the exception of three persons living in Hong Kong, Chen Chao-Bo, Yu Shao-chi and Yang Ho-lin, and one man at Shanghai, Lu Ko-tung. The others avoided me, as a rebel, as they would one stricken with the plague.
>
> Living together with my three friends, Chen, Yu and Yang, in Hong Kong, we were constantly discussing the revolution. Our thoughts were fixed on the problems of the Chinese revolution. We studied chiefly the history of revolutions. . . .[3]

These were also years when there began the friendship between the young medical student and his English teacher, Dr Cantlie, and Mrs Cantlie. It was to be deep and lasting, and of great historical importance. Sun had been, academically speaking, a good student. But it was evidently something much more than his medical knowledge, his 'skill, coolness of judgment and dexterity' as a surgeon which made Cantlie visit Sun in Macao. Many years later he tried to explain what it was that made him love and respect Sun: 'His is a nature that draws men's regard towards him and makes them ready to serve him at the operating-table or on the battlefield; an unexplainable influence, a magnetism.'[4]

In 1892 Sun had begun the formation of an organization which he called the Revive China Society. After he left Macao he went to Canton. There he and his Choyhung fellow-rebel decided to draw up a memorandum on reforms which were necessary, and to present them to the Viceroy of Chihli (now Hopei) province in the north, Li Hung-chang. This official not only held one of the highest positions in the land, but he had also a reputation as a person of unusual intelligence and ability, very concerned about China's problems. Sun must have hoped that some of the ideas he had for China's regeneration could be tried out if he could get a man like Li interested. The journey to Tientsin was a long one, and the two young men would have to walk and travel where possible by boat. But they did set out, and get to Tientsin, and returned after going to Peking and the Yangtze area. It was Sun's first visit outside his native province, except for the visits to Amoy.

Li Hung-chang does not appear to have been interested in the proposals for reform, and it is not certain if he even took the trouble to look at them. Sun's scientific education appears to have led him to write about resource development, about research into agriculture and the use of machines, and the kind of education which would enable the Chinese to use what talents they had in order to modernize China. That Sun should have paid attention to 'the improvement of agriculture' is interesting. Sun's proposals may not have made a hit with the august Viceroy of Chihli, but a year later there seems to have been enough interest in them for someone to put them into print. For the two budding revolutionaries the journey was an education. Moving among the common people in the towns and the country-side, discovering what variety and potential there was among the Chinese (for most of China was unlike Kwang-tung), Sun and his friend must have come to see that the kind of reforms proposed in the memorial to Li would not

22

solve China's problems, and were in any case inadequate. The Manchus and the whole corrupt and outdated apparatus of rule they maintained by force had to be got rid of, before the long-delayed and difficult tasks of agricultural and industrial modernization could be attended to.

Sun's conviction led him in 1894 to begin serious work building up the Revive China Society. Money, arms, soldiers and organizers were necessary. The Chinese who had emigrated, and were therefore beyond the reach of the Manchu police and officials, could help him without endangering themselves. He started off on a world tour. But he had only got as far as Honolulu, where his brother Te-chang lived, when he was called back by his colleagues. The Chinese Empire had suffered a crushing defeat at the hands of the well-organized army and navy of the rising imperial power, Japan. It was a disaster for the Chinese and the time had come for the revolutionaries to act. In September 1895 Sun was in Canton with his colleagues; they gathered their forces for their attempt to overthrow the imperial government and inaugurate, as they thought, a new era in Chinese history.

NOTES

1. Li Chien-nung, *The Political History of China 1840–1928*. Tr. and ed. by Jeremy Ingalls and Ssu-yu Teng, Stanford University Press 1967, p. 165.

2. Sun Yat-sen, *Memoirs of a Revolutionary*. Quoted in Franz Schurmann and Orville Schell, *Republican China*, Penguin Books 1968, p. 11.

3. Ibid., p. 11.

4. James Cantlie and C. Sheridan Jones, *Sun Yat-sen and the Awakening of China*, Jarrolds, nd, p. 42.

3   Nineteenth-Century China

Talk of revolution is so commonplace today that it may appear unnecessary to pay special attention to the fact that Sun became a professional revolutionary. It is respectable to discourse on revolution, join left-wing groups, and take part in demonstrations against the established order. Newspapers, which nearly all actively work to strengthen the established order, discuss the finer points of disputes among left-wing sects, and the most bitter and violent denunciations of the ruling class often get wide publicity. Talk about revolution tends to bore people, not frighten them, as serious revolutionary practice would. A society in which the ruling class is in command of the political, material and cultural means which secure their power encourages it. For it acts as a safety valve, develops talents which would be useful, and provides useful criticisms.

In China in the last years of the nineteenth century people often got together to talk secretly about the need for change. But it was far from fashionable to be a revolutionary. The government was so insecure that it could not have tolerated with impunity the spread of ideas of how its power could be overthrown. It knew that it could not count on the loyalty of the mass of the people, and particularly on sections of Chinese society which could, if they wished, create an independent centre of power in China: the intellectuals, as we would call them today; the labouring classes, especially the peasants; and the soldiers. A careful watch was kept for any talk or activity which could turn the disaffection into active revolt. Revolutionaries – that is, those who united and worked so that the mass of the people could set up a more just political and economic order – had in this respect as much difficulty as serious revolutionaries anywhere else. They also had difficulties which were peculiar to the Chinese society of that period. Readers may be familiar with the features of late nineteenth-century China referred to. But it would still be useful for us to look briefly at the historical situation which spoke to Sun and his colleagues of the urgent need for revolution. That situation provides the setting for our story, and explains the immensity of the task which was being undertaken by anyone who was seeking to lead the Chinese to work for their own salvation as a people.

That conditions in China were bad was widely acknowledged. High officials, and even some members of the imperial court, were to be found among those who wanted to know what reforms the government should undertake. There was little agreement, however, on what was wrong in China and on what needed to be done. During the short period in his youth when Sun worked as a peasant in Choyhung he tried to stir up his elders by his political talk. But it must have dawned on him then that it was not the corrupt and inefficient rulers and officials alone who were the problem; how the people of China could be brought to look critically and rationally at their situation was also a problem. Oppression, even when it is most painful and destructive, can be successful if what its victims are persuaded to believe and think makes them submit to the people who are taxing, robbing, enslaving and violating them in other ways. Sun's iconoclasm was not appreciated at all by the people of Choyhung. In a revolution there would be things other than the Son of Heaven (the Emperor), more difficult and more important, to be thrown down. In China it was not (as in Europeanized societies) 'Christian' superstitions through which the human spirit – with its creative vigour and daring – was fettered and poisoned. The Chinese had their indigenous forms of religious superstition.

The fact that some Chinese, out of their own experience

and on their own initiative, were beginning to work for revolutionary change was itself of great historic importance. Something radically new was growing out of Chinese soil. Were more revolutionaries going to spring from the hundreds of thousands of village communities which for thousands of years had maintained the stability of Chinese society? The notion of what it was to be Chinese seemed to exclude the possibility of revolution. To be a good Chinese one had to learn to respect the hierarchy of authority and obedience, from the Emperor down to the young girls. It was the observance of the traditional pattern of authority within the state, within the village, within the clan, and within the family, which had preserved China through the rise and fall of dynasties. It was understandable that at a time when China was fighting for her survival many people would want to cling to tradition, not join in fighting it. They would not be inclined to become 'bandits' or to join with the men from overseas who did not respect the principles of civilized behaviour, the 'barbarians' who had already done so much harm to China.

The problems of winning moral authority for the creation of a 'new' China was difficult enough at that time. To it was added the problem of organizing and uniting revolutionaries over a country of continental proportions. Sun, for example, was authentically Chinese because he was a native of Kwangtung. He could not easily understand, or be understood by, his compatriots in the majority of provinces. It was only by discovering what the Chinese people in the widely-scattered villages and provinces wanted to achieve that he could be in a position to organize the countrywide revolution on the correct lines. In the early nineteenth century China proper had stretched from the borders of Nepal and Kashmir to the western shores of the North Pacific. Even though the Russians had subsequently annexed a vast deal of Chinese territory the geographical difficulties in organizing an underground revolutionary organization were great enough to deter most people who wanted to end Manchu rule.

What it is that drives people to revolutionary activity is not always easy to explain with precision. It certainly is not psychological instability or personal frustration, as some cruder counter-revolutionary theories of our day try to suggest. Nor is it the prospect, generally, of material rewards. In Sun's case a lucrative career as a doctor or a businessman was well within his reach. If we may anticipate the study a little and speak of Sun's quite unusual talents and his tremendous energy, we would not be too far out if we assumed that if Sun had taken the single step to a bourgeois existence which would have made him a westernized Chinese gentleman, he could have achieved international distinction. It is not an abstract idealism which made him choose to be a 'bandit'. We may say with truth that what Sun knew to be the aspirations and deserts of the Chinese people – victims both of a despotic regime and of foreign aggression – made the decision for him.

4   A Revolutionary in Exile

The Treaty of Shimonoseki (April 1895) ended the war which Japan had begun the previous year. The Chinese were forced to let the Japanese have the Liaotung Peninsula, Taiwan and the Pescadores. (The Japanese had earlier taken the Liu-chu, or Ryuuku, Islands.) Though the Japanese had been the aggressors, the Chinese had, according to the precedent established in their dealings with the other capitalist powers, to pay an enormous 'indemnity' to Japan. The Chinese had also to let the Japanese occupy Korea, which had formerly looked to China for protection. Many Chinese, including Sun, blamed the Chinese government (and with justification) for accepting this humiliation and the loss of a part of China.

Sun's associates had asked him to hurry back because the moment seemed right for their uprising. Demobilized soldiers from the war areas were roaming the countryside, terrorizing the peasants. People seemed unaware of the calamity that threatened China – its break-up among the greedy imperial powers which had already partitioned Africa among themselves. China was threatened not only by Britain, France, Belgium, Germany, Russia and other European powers, but in addition by Japan and the United States. The appeal of the Revive China Society, worded cautiously so as not to arouse too much government curiosity about its revolutionary aims, had spoken of a national emergency even before China's defeat in 1895:

> . . . Our strong neighbours look down upon us and despise us for the reason that we are not one at heart. Our people are striving for selfish and immediate ends, and neglect the situation in the large.

They do not realize that when China is one day dismembered by other people their sons and grandsons will be enslaved and their families will go unprotected. There can be no urgency more urgent than this. Selfishness was never more selfish. The whole nation is confused. . . . How then is calamity to be averted? If we do not make an effort to hold our own, if we do not rouse ourselves in time, our thousands of years of fame and culture, our many generations of traditions and morals, will be destroyed, utterly ruined.

There is no ready-made prescription for dealing with a complex situation such as the one in which Sun's colleagues and followers waited for him to give a lead. They all had to learn how they were going to overthrow Manchu rule and open up a bright future for China. They believed that if they seized the provincial government headquarters in Canton, and won over some of the government troops, they could march north, eventually taking Peking. As a cover for their plot they started an Agricultural Association, with branches in Canton and Hong Kong. To outsiders, enthusiasm for innovations in agriculture appeared to be the cause of the tremendous activity which went on in Hong Kong and Canton; actually, arms and ammunition were being bought, and together with a small band of soldiers, being smuggled into Canton. But something went wrong at the last moment; it was, probably, the fact that a crate or barrel belonging to a consignment marked 'Cement' fell and broke open, alerting the police to the fact that arms were being smuggled in. Lu Hao-tung persuaded Sun to leave, but he himself was caught in the office. He had been Sun's close comrade since their small revolt in Choyhung against superstition, and he had put all the money he could raise into the attempt to take Canton. He met the fate to which the Manchus consigned all rebels – execution.

Sun was now a wanted man, but none of the people among whom he hid or with whom he made the journey to Hong Kong betrayed him. This was a demonstration of the remarkable skill for disguise and disappearance which was to serve him well for the rest of his life. Advised by friends to leave Hong Kong, he went to Japan and then to the Philippines. He found that members of his society were disheartened by the failure, and there was not sufficient support for him to plan another uprising. The British authorities had banned his entry into Hong Kong. He decided therefore to continue the worldwide visits to Chinese communities overseas, which he had begun before he was called back in the spring.

Chinese emigrants were to be found in Hawaii, in the United States and in South East Asia. Many of them were traders and coolies who had no cause to love the Manchu regime. Sun was disappointed with the apathetic attitude of his compatriots. But he was perhaps expecting more from them than he had reason to. Some of his comrades who had sacrificed their careers and their lives for the revolutionary cause were exceptional men; and they had been with him for years. It was remarkable that his brother, who continued to prosper in Honolulu, was so keen a supporter of his cause. Their mother and sister, and Sun's wife (to whom he had been married when they were still boy and girl) and their children had all to flee Choyhung to escape Manchu 'justice', and it was Te-chang who provided a home for all of them.

Sun's passionate devotion to the cause of China's regeneration, his uncanny powers of persuasion, and the evident deterioration in China's condition all helped him to gain some new support. But he realized that he could not rush things if he was to hope for success on his second attempt. On his travels he not only carried on revolutionary agitation among groups of Chinese of all classes, but also read and studied extensively, working out plans for a regenerated China. The policies for technological and scientific modernization and for revolutionary change in education and training which he had first outlined to the Viceroy of Chihli were obviously not going to be carried out by officials of the Empire. They would have to be hammered out by the revolutionaries when they had got rid of the corrupt and reactionary mandarins. Sun was acting on the assumption that it was up to the Chinese themselves to explore what was being thought and done all over the world, and to make up their own minds on what should be done in their country. He was at the beginning of his career too obscure a person for the foreigners who had power over China to worry about. His was just the name of a much-wanted 'bandit'. Or he appeared as an idealist who need not enter into the calculations of those whose job it was to see that imperial interests in China would remain permanently and continue to flourish.

Sun's travels took him across the United States and then to Britain. He had earlier, on reaching Japan, cut off his queue (a symbol of Chinese subjection to the Manchu minority) and had grown a moustache. His appearance had changed, and when his friends the Cantlie's had met him in Honolulu, wearing European-styled clothes, they had not at first recognized him. But the spies of the imperial government were on his trail, and his arrival in London was discovered. On Sunday, 11 October, Sun was on his way from his lodgings to join the Cantlie's and attend service at St Martin-in-the-Fields, when he was kidnapped and imprisoned in the Chinese Legation. It was the plan of Sir Halliday Macartney, an Englishman who was Secretary at the Legation, to have the rebel leader illegally shipped to China; there he would meet the slow death by torture which was his due.

For Sun the days which passed, as the arrangements for smuggling him out of Britain were made, were a time of deep personal crisis. The oppressive government, to the destruction of which he had dedicated his life, was going to make sure that the abortive uprising of 1895 would be his last piece of work. He had allowed himself to be captured too easily. These could not have been all the thoughts that troubled Sun during those 'days of suffering'. He was a man of supreme physical as well as moral courage, but anticipation of having to submit helplessly to torture or execution must have been painful for him. At times like this when the human spirit is severely tested, it has happened that even men of great integrity admit defeat. Sun came through the crisis with a renewed sense of the mission to which he had been ordained.

The almost miraculous powers of persuasion which he had proved equal to the difficulties. One of his English guards agreed to smuggle out news of his imprisonment. Dr Cantlie, getting an anonymous note one night, discovered what had happened to his friend. He acted at once. His attempts to reach officials in the local police station and at Scotland Yard were of no avail; whether it was just inefficiency or whether the alleged kidnapping of a Chinaman did not bother the guardians of the law it is difficult to say. A detective had to be employed to watch the Legation, while Cantlie and a friend of his carried on their campaign to get Sun released. It was six days after they began that the Foreign Office acted, and Macartney was forced to let Sun go free.

A kidnapping which had resulted in intervention by the Prime Minister, Lord Salisbury, naturally roused much public interest in the young revolutionary from China. There was some controversy in the correspondence columns of *The Times*. Britain at that time was still the world's leading power, and her rulers were sure enough of themselves not to worry too much about the presence in the country of revolutionaries, provided they did not break the law. Liberals influenced public opinion, and Britons tended to be sympathetic to peoples who were struggling against despotic rule by non-British regimes. Apart from those who had a vested interest in preventing the regeneration of China, people had little to say on behalf of Manchu despotism.

Sun later wrote:

After escaping from London, I went to Europe to study the methods of its political administration, and also to make the acquaintance of representatives of the opposition parties. In Europe I understood that, although the foremost European countries had achieved power and popular government, they could not accord complete happiness to their peoples. Therefore the leading European revolutionaries strive for a social revolution, and I conceived the idea of the simultaneous settlement, by means of the revolution, of the questions of national economy, national independence, and popular freedom. Hence arose my so-called '*san-min-chu-i*', or the idea of democracy based on three principles.

The revolution was my principal aim in life, and therefore I hastened to conclude my business in Europe, in order not to lose time dear to the revolution. I left for Japan, considering that there, nearer to China, we could more successfully carry out our revolutionary plans. . . .[1]

It was probably a year or more after his London visit that Sun reached Japan. He must have been very busy in Europe, for he appears to have read and thought a great deal, and got to know what it was like for the mass of the people who lived in the other great civilization area to his own, Europe. There had been a time when nearly all the most advanced books in the world that a Chinese statesman needed to read could be found in China. But China had for some centuries not been contributing to human advances in technology, politics, economics and philosophy, and had not even kept up with modern developments that, almost from decade to decade, were changing the world. It would have to be one of the aims of a revolution to end the backwardness which the decadent ruling classes had imposed on the Chinese. Sun's intensive reading in European libraries was a necessary self-education which he could not have got in Hong Kong or even in Japan.

Sun lived simply. He saw much of that side of European cities which tourists and distinguished visitors from other continents do not normally see. The behaviour, ideas and values of Europeans and Americans in China and other

Asian countries had left much to be desired. The misery of the poor in Europe, the way in which the ruling classes regarded the mass of their own people and exploited them, the backwardness of the very classes of people who produced the great wealth of Europe and the United States, and the arguments and political analyses of revolutionaries in Europe, must have had a profound effect on Sun. Through their impact on him these social realities were to have an impact on the Chinese people. It is difficult even today to appreciate Sun's genius – the boldness and originality of his leadership. Seventy years ago Sun saw clearly what some Third World leaders are discovering only now, that westernization was no solution for the problems they were called upon to solve, and was not necessary for the advance in the development of the non-western peoples. 'To make a nation rich and strong, or to promote democracy as has been done in European nations, was not sufficient to make people really happy.'

Sun knew that during those very years that he spent struggling over the ideological and practical issues there were campaigns in China for reforms 'from above' on bureaucratic lines. There was Kang Yu-wei (like Sun a man from Kwangtung, but eight years older) who was making a bid to be a new-style mandarin. There was Liang Chi-chao, Kang's disciple, later to be much praised by the 'old China hands' among scholars from the imperialist countries. There were men like the western-educated Yen Fu, who advocated a superficial westernization, and later became anti-western reactionaries. Kang Yu-wei was to have his moment of glory when for a short period the Emperor adopted his proposals, and issued a series of edicts, in 1898. Sun, on the other hand, could look with detachment at both traditions – that of the Chinese élites and that of the ruling classes of the European countries. He saw that China would have to have her own revolution in the '*people*'s livelihood' in order to achieve the needed transformation in politics and

34

in society. She would have to chart and follow a new path of her own; she would have to learn from the achievements as well as the serious failures of the 'early developers' (to use the jargon of our own day), and not blindly follow people with a different history.

The year or two in Europe at the end of the nineteenth century only began a new development in Sun's thinking. It will be relevant to recall what those years were in the history of the European revolutionary movements. When Sun was in Europe, Lenin (four years his junior) was serving his sentence of exile, his first political imprisonment, in Siberia. Keen debates were being conducted about the revolutionary possibilities in the less industrialized countries, about terrorism, peaceful transition and violent struggle. In 1896, the year Sun was in London, the Second International had held its Congress in London. When Sun wrote later that '(he) learned a great deal from what (he) saw and heard', what encounters was he recalling? Did his sensitive and alert mind catch all the nuances of the political controversies among the Marxists and other revolutionaries from all over Europe who met to discuss and plan the future of capitalism? Was this citizen of the Manchu-ruled, imperialist-dominated 'middle kingdom' tempted to linger in the exciting and exhilarating atmosphere of European revolutionary thought? We do not know. It he was tempted, he resisted the temptation. For he was conscious of how different the situation was for the Chinese, for whom the terms 'working class', 'bourgeoisie' and 'capitalism' had at that time little meaning, and for whom the controversies about the French Revolution, the Communist Manifesto, Bakunin and various other thinkers would at best be academic.

China had developed for millennia as a sort of federation of village communities held together by a common administration and a common civilization. It needed urgently to achieve unity as a nation, *at the level of the people*. Sun was acutely conscious, and rightly so, of the great importance of developing a political identity among the people. For a people oppressed internally and also by the capitalist nation-states through their highly centralized power, *collective* action was necessary. This was one of the earliest arguments for the revolutionary nationalism which in years to come was to achieve the liberation of peoples subjected to both despotic rule and colonial exploitation.

Sun's conception of the solidarity of the Chinese people was a progressive one, and in no way was a barrier to the development of genuine internationalism. 'Narrow patriotism' was something he warned against. A few years later he was saying:

Our country must not be considered as the property of any private individual. Moreover, at present foreigners are preying on China. More than ever is the establishment of a strong government necessary and this can only be the government of the whole people. . . . Commensurate with the growth of the economic power of the western countries is the growth of the misery of the people. In England, for instance, there are a few rich, but many poor people. This is because the human elements cannot resist the capitalistic forces. . . . Industrial civilization has advantages and inconveniences, but the rich in Europe and America have monopolized the former, leaving to the poor the latter. Such a social condition is tending to develop in China, but if we know how to act preventatively, the struggle against capitalism will be easier than in the West. . . . We want the national revolution of independence because we don't want any one person to monopolize all political power. We want the social revolution because we don't want a handful of rich people to monopolize the whole wealth of the country. Failure in any one of these three aims means the failure of our mission. Only when all three aims are attained can the Chinese be proud of their country.

Those words were from a speech Sun made to 5,000 members of the revolutionary organization he was to found in 1905; the speech was made, Bernard Martin, who quotes from it, tells us, in 1907.[2] What progress had the revolutionaries made in the intervening years towards their goal of creating a new China? In China the 'Hundred Days' Reform', as it came to be called, came to an end when the

36

masterful Empress Dowager reasserted her power over the weak-willed Emperor, her son. Kang Yu-wei, and others of the conservative reformers who did not get arrested, fled for their lives. The reactionary Manchu nobles had the support of many old-style scholars who saw the reforms which the Emperor had tried to introduce as threats to their careers. As Sun and his colleagues made arrangements for their second revolutionary attempt the court, the officials and the military chiefs were leading China willy-nilly on the road to disaster.

NOTES

1. *Memoirs of a Revolutionary*, p. 12.
2. Martin, op. cit., p. 109.

5 The Formation of the Revolutionary United League

At the time of the Sino-Japanese War of 1894–5 the danger of the break-up of China was very real. The series of 'unequal treaties' which had been forced on China ever since the First Opium War of 1838–42 had revealed very clearly the fact that the international order was based not on universally valid principles but on force and fraud. Just as weak and unprotected people are an obvious prey for gangsters, so China, once its pretensions to greatness and power were shown to be hollow, roused the greed and rapacity of capitalists who were using their control of the governments and armed forces of the European countries, Japan and the United States, to secure monopolies of territory, markets, raw material resources and military outposts in the lands of weaker peoples.

Although this form of aggression has gone on for a long time, and is obviously being practised today, some readers may find plain speaking about it rather offensive. The practice of the British, Spanish, French, Dutch, American, Japanese and other expansionist governments has been more than merely offensive to several generations of non-European peoples. It has been ruinous, humiliating and, in some cases, fatal. Though it appears almost impossible for people in the imperialist countries to see their own actions from the viewpoint of the peoples whose lands they have attacked, invaded and occupied, the attempt must be made to enter into the feelings and thoughts of the people who paid the cost of the creation of the worldwide capitalist order – the first truly global economic and political order. The word *xenophobia* has in recent years been used in the propaganda of western Asian 'scholars' to suggest that that has been a national characteristic of the Chinese. That is, to speak simply, a lie. The reaction of the Chinese (like other peoples who were subject to similar experiences) to the peoples who invaded and occupied their country, killed and raped, plundered resources and seized territory was complex. But it was generally the right one – one of hostility and determination to get rid of the foreign oppressors. That was not xenophobia. Attacks on the foreigners who had done to China what they *had* in fact done in the nineteenth century are not to be compared to attacks on, or an expression of hatred for, peoples of other nations and civilizations who are carrying on their legitimate occupations. The mounting fury of the Chinese had been built up not against the Britons in Britain, the Russians in Russia or the French in France. It was directed against violent intruders whose conduct was hateful and whose presence was intolerable.

The Manchus, though they were natives of China, were a minority who treated the rest of the Chinese as inferiors. Their lack of sympathy for what the majority of Chinese felt about their disgrace and impotence only added to the latter's frustration. After the partition of Africa, China was the only major area of the world left for the greedy imperialist powers to fight over or divide. The Russians had seized enormous areas of north China; they had moved in in a systematic way, massacring the Chinese populations where they resisted, and imposing on the Peking government, powerless to resist, 'treaties' by which they surrendered hundreds of thousands of square miles of land. They coveted China's north-eastern provinces and her borderlands in the far West. The Japanese had not only seized territory, but they also forced the Peking government to agree to their setting up their factories in China – thereby taking China a step nearer to full colonial status. Her rivals, however, put pressure on her to withdraw from the Liaotung Peninsula, a strategic position from which she could have threatened not only Tientsin but the imperialist activities of the other powers. The Germans then demanded Kiaochow Bay in Shantung province, the French Kwanghow Bay, the British Weihaiwei and the Russians Port Arthur. The Chinese government obliged!

Apart from the Japanese, the foreigners in possession or occupation of various parts of China manifested a great concern for the Christian religion, as they defined it. The activities of missionaries, who had been accorded privileged status by the hated unequal treaties, were understandably seen as part of the foreign aggression. The missionaries had not sought entry to China as guests. Chinese who became Christians were treated by the missionaries as their protégés, and were consequently regarded locally as people who collaborated with the foreign aggressors. Christian Germany had forcibly occupied Kiaochow Bay in Shantung because two German missionaries in China had been murdered.

Radical elements among the Chinese masses accepted the logic of these practices. They expressed their resentment against foreign imperialists and Christians by attacking them. The target of their attacks included the Manchu regime, but ultra-conservatives found a way of saving themselves and preventing the uprising from becoming a revolutionary one by encouraging the anti-foreign elements. Started by the *I-ho-tuan* (Righteous and Harmonious Society) the uprising, known in the West as the Boxer Uprising, was a strange mixture of progressive and reactionary political attitudes. It was in Shantung that it began, and it eventually reached Peking, where the foreign legations had established themselves. The movement rose out of deeply-felt opposition to what the foreigners were doing in and to China, but it was badly conceived and led, and was deflected from its main purposes into a series of savage

and politically meaningless activities. The Christian governments responded in force and defeated the Boxers, their
troops indulging in an orgy of murder, rape and destruction which seemed almost to be aimed at validating all that
the Boxers said about the foreigners. (Some missionaries
were dissatisfied with what they considered the light
punishment given to the Chinese.) The military expedition to
relieve the Legation Quarter in Peking had been necessary
and justified. But the use to which the foreign powers put the
Boxer Uprising was significant. Foreign troops were stationed in Tientsin and Peking, and heavy 'indemnities'
imposed on the Chinese – indemnities which obviously
meant that the desperately poor Chinese peasants would be
taxed more heavily than ever to enrich those who were
ruining their country. The Russians, who had used the
events of 1899–1900 to move their troops in force into
China's north-eastern provinces, remained there and would
not budge. Their insatiable greed for territory was, as
events were to show, making them rash.

These events could not fail to affect the revolutionaries.
The peasants, miserably armed, had fought with fantastic
courage, not for any gain, but for China against its foreign
enemies, or those who appeared to them to be enemies. Sun
was in Japan at this time. The Hsing Chung Hui was having
problems because sharp practice by members of the reform-
er's Emperor Protection Society was causing his own support to fall off. 'The most difficult period of my entire
revolutionary career,' said Sun of these years, writing just
after the 1911 Revolution. 'During this time there appeared
the Emperor Protection Society, which fought against
revolution and republicanism for the Ching much more
vigorously than the dynasty itself.'[1]

Japan at this time had only started its career as an imperialist power of the western type. There were differences
among the Japanese themselves about the role Japan, the
rising non-European power, should play in world affairs.

There were Japanese liberals and socialists who wanted to ally themselves with progressive forces, and it was the hope of the Chinese, Filipino and other revolutionaries to get help from Japan. The question whether foreign assistance should be sought in the waging of a revolutionary struggle is a difficult one to answer. If foreigners are prepared to provide aid which is asked for and to refrain from trying to take over the running of the struggle, their aid might be worth getting. But, even in that case, there might be a price to be paid in the way of special privileges to be granted to the aid-givers in the event of success. Sun and his colleagues found many Japanese very helpful, but they had to be careful that they were not being used by expansionist elements.

The second revolutionary attempt under Sun's leadership reached its climax in October 1900. It was timed to take place when the Peking government was preoccupied with the Boxer Uprising. Japanese help was essential for the success of the undertaking, and the possibility of success was very real. What actually happened is so complicated that any brief narrative of what happened will only confuse the reader. The tangled motives of the Japanese in the plot, added to those of the Chinese with whom Sun was allied, made it impossible for the rebellion to be completed according to plan. Sun was kept busy travelling back and forth; he had to meet people in Singapore, Hong Kong, Canton, Taiwan and Japan. So many forces were involved or almost involved. He did not want to depend exclusively on Japanese goodwill. He made an attempt to get the British in Hong Kong to take a neutral stand in the event of a revolutionary war; he told them what sort of regime he would set up and what its programme would be. The British not only ignored Sun's proposals but also banned his entry into Hong Kong!

The attempts to overthrow the Empire and set up a republic did not cease. There was to be another longish interval before the third attempt under Sun's direction, in

42

August 1906. That, too, failed, as did subsequent attempts in May 1907, September 1907, December 1907, April 1908, February 1910 and April 1911. It was not until October 1911 that the regime was finally toppled from power, In the intervening years Sun was a man with a vast price on his head, a notorious revolutionary, a man with no country and almost no home. His reputation with the imperialist powers was such that he had been banned entry into British, Dutch and French territories adjoining China. He was unwelcome in Japan. There were periods when he disappeared, and assumed disguises which enabled him to enter China and carry on his work there.

The government had an efficient secret police and spy network, which had been developed to cope with the activities of the secret societies. The high rewards offered for the capture or assassination of this 'bandit' would have tempted many people to bring Sun's career to an end. Rewards totalling £100,000 must have made Sun's capture worth the while of even the richest men. Sun had great personal courage and presence of mind, and only a few of his adventures are known. Dr Cantlie related a few of them in his book. Sun did much of his secret travelling within China on foot or by junk, and for safety lived on board junks.

Once at Nanking a man entered Sun's cabin on board a junk and announced that he had been offered $5,000 to effect his capture. Sun reasoned with the would-be captor, with the result that the man fell at his feet in an agony of repentance and implored pardon. The man desisted. Why? Sun's personality merely, for he was not armed. No one who has come in close touch with Sun Yat-sen has not felt the magic of his presence. . . . The betrayer in this instance . . . went and hanged himself, as he could not face the world again after having even thought of giving up Sun to his enemies. . . .

One of the most serious attempts on his life was made by two young government officials, attended by a dozen soldiers, in Canton. They entered Sun's room late one evening. The position was desperate, for his capture or death would mean promotion and high rewards to these officers. Even then did Sun's calmness effect his safety. Apprised of their advent, he took up one of the sacred books on the table beside him and read aloud. The would-be captors listened and then began to ask questions. Sun entered into conversation with them, and in two hours' time the officials with their attendant soldiers departed.[2]

Sun's power over people was nothing magical or mystical. The Cantlie's, who could not have understood Sun's views and ideology in the abstract (his republicanism alone was difficult for them to swallow), could see that Sun's seriousness and selflessness was the expression of the tremendous social and spiritual force of the Chinese people. Sun lived in such a way that his continued existence was in itself his mandate to lead the Chinese people. The coolies, boatmen, fishermen, peasants and soldiers who hid him and protected him did not allow him to be betrayed because they knew that here at last was a Chinese leader who would not betray the people once they had made him and his colleagues the new leaders of China. By a political process more valid than formal election, Sun had been 'voted' China's leader long before the façade of Manchu power collapsed.

With or without Sun's presence, the political work and organization essential for revolutionary success went on ceaselessly. The support for the conservatives and reformers declined, and that for the Tung-Meng Hui (the revolutionary organization which replaced the Hsing Chung Hui) grew. Returned students from overseas, officers and men in the imperial armies and navy, coolies, merchants and even officials were either members of, or were ready to serve, the Tung-Meng Hui. The transformation of the Chinese people was an essential part of the revolutionary process. Foreign observers and residents, who had often got used to speaking of the Chinese in the foulest and most insulting terms, saw only the corruption and cowardice in high places, and the signs of meanness and servility in those who had succumbed to poverty, racial contempt, violence and their own fear.

But the new hope and determination, the desire to join Sun in creating a new China, spread over the country almost unnoticed by foreigners.

Sun's work kept him busy outside China much of the time. The different groups working for the same end had to be welded together. Political workers had to be trained in the principles of the revolution. The very trying demands of diplomacy between the Tung-Meng Hui and foreign governments had to be met with a cool and clear head. Money and arms were needed, and facilities for the printing and distribution of publications. The study of tactics, especially military tactics, was essential; Sun was interested in the guerrilla tactics used by the Boers. Military training had to be organized, and conducted with due secrecy. After the Boxer Uprising the flow of Chinese students abroad increased. Many more went to Japan than any other country, but the numbers who went to Europe were not negligible. The new wave of students tended also to be younger than those in the past, who had often been sent to Japan to complete training begun in China.

Japan was at this time going through a critical phase in her political development, and students and other Chinese living in Japan could not help being deeply affected by the attitude of the Japanese. The continued Russian occupation of the north-eastern provinces had angered the Chinese, and the students had demonstrated in favour of a war to expel the Russians. The Japanese, too, had been provoked by the Russian action, though for reasons which the Chinese could not applaud. The expansionists had criticized the government for the fact that after the Boxer Uprising the Japanese had got no territorial gains whereas Russia had. In 1902 the Japanese entered into an alliance with the British, and in 1904–5, in their war with Russia, there was the first major clash between two imperialist powers. Among the Chinese, and among other colonial and semi-colonial peoples who had resented the white racism which had grown out of

European world-domination, the defeat of a European power by Asians was widely celebrated.

The Chinese in Japan, while they admired Japan's ability to hold its own with the major powers, did not enjoy the experience of being patronized and obstructed by the Japanese. For the Japanese government tended to be less and less influenced by the liberals who admired Sun. In fact, it became increasingly anxious about the effect on Japanese politics of the radical and socialist ideas of some of the members of the Tung-Meng Hui. Their organization of a revolution by the Chinese people, and therefore by the peasants, went far beyond the admiration that some anti-Manchu nationalists had at first had for Japan's ability to modernize herself. All these suspicions and fears of the Japanese added to the difficulties of the revolutionary leaders, who were using Yokohama (a port which gave easy access to China) as their headquarters. In 1907 the Japanese expelled Sun, and ever after that not only the spies employed by the imperial Chinese government but those of the Japanese government, too, watched Sun as he travelled all over the world.

But before his enforced departure from Japan in 1907, Sun had made a tour of North America and Europe which had turned out to be important. He set out late in 1903, stopping in Hawaii and then going on to the United States, where he spent a year. The meetings and discussions which could not be conducted in China could be held freely among the Chinese living, visiting or studying abroad. Sun was often exhausted by the amount of work he did, but he appears to have been able to rouse people out of their lethargy. He was interested in hearing what other Chinese thought and felt about China, and wanted to see done. The serious discussion of the future of the 'great' Chinese Empire with people engaged in menial occupations, far from seeming ridiculous in Sun's eyes, was done as part of his work as the leader of the revolution.

46

In Europe there were Chinese student communities in London, Brussels, Paris and Berlin. In his meetings with these students in 1905 Sun found it possible to develop his Three Principles. He also began the formation of the revolutionary Tung-Meng Hui. This is how Sun told the story in later years:

In the spring of 1905 I arrived in Europe once again, and the majority of students there were supporters of the revolution. They had only just arrived in Europe from Japan or China. The revolutionary wave seized them, and they soon began to go on from arguments about the revolution to direct revolutionary activities. I then set forth my long-guarded ideas about democracy embodied in three principles and the 'Fivefold Constitution', in order to create a revolutionary organization on their basis. Our first meeting took place at Brussels, and thirty people entered our league. The second meeting was organized in Berlin, and there twenty-odd persons joined. The third meeting was in Paris, where ten people entered the league; but at the fourth meeting in Tokyo several hundred new members joined. There were in our league representatives of all the provinces of China, with the exception of Kansu, as Kansu had not yet sent any students to Japan. At the time our league was being set up the word 'revolution' was still terrifying, and therefore our league was simply called the 'United League'. . . .

After the creation of the United League, I began to believe that a new era of the Chinese Revolution was opening before us. Previously, I had more than once met with great difficulties. I had been spat upon and ridiculed by all. I more than once suffered defeats, but I audaciously moved forward, although I must confess I did not dream of the accomplishment of the overthrow of the Manchu Dynasty in my lifetime. However, from the autumn of 1905 onward, after the creation of the revolutionary United League, I became convinced that the great cause of the Chinese Revolution would be accomplished during my lifetime. . . . Scarcely a year had passed before ten thousand people joined our United League. Branches were organized in almost all of the provinces, and from this time forward the revolutionary movement went ahead with great strides. Its further development exceeded all my anticipations. . . .[3]

While Sun was away from Japan another distinguished revolutionary leader, a young Hunanese named Huang Hsing, had escaped to Japan after leading an unsuccessful revolt. A man of great courage and resourcefulness, Huang Hsing was becoming a legend himself. Sun met him for the first time when he returned to Japan. The two men became friends and worked together to effect the formal organization of the United League. Huang Hsing became deputy leader of the revolutionary movement, and Sun, who was never after personal power, trusted Huang Hsing to take the necessary initiatives and direct affairs. There were others with whom Sun shared leadership responsibilities, among them Hu Han-min and Sung Chiao-jen.

The manifesto of the Tung-Meng Hui was drawn up partly in order to serve as propaganda for the movement. It was drawn up in the form of a proclamation to be made on the occasion of an uprising. It spoke of the glorious rebellions of the past, and pointed to the new character of the present revolution: 'If former times there were heroes' revolutions, today we have a revolution of the people. "National revolution" means that all the people in the nation . . . will all bear the responsibility of revolution.' Republicanism, it made clear, was not merely the replacement of the Emperor by a President. It was as equals that the people established a republican government, and chose from among themselves a President and a parliament.

One cannot emphasize too much how remarkable this was as a serious platform for the creation of a new order in China. Many of the students and others in Japan and Europe were sons of members of the 'gentry' in China – people who owned land and had tenants who paid exorbitant rents; some must have been sons of officials. Yet they followed Sun in affirming that essential to all the ways and means they might use in transforming the livelihood of the people and the national polity was freedom, equality and fraternity. The commitment to land reform was even more revolutionary. The oath taken by members of the Tung-Meng Hui was a solemn one and binding; in a country where secret societies were common the severe penalties for

48

violating the oath were understood. And members swore not only to overthrow the Manchus and set up a republic, but also to equalize land distribution.

The programme of the United League was advanced even by European standards. No wonder it stirred the people as students and others carried news of what was happening throughout China. The peasants who had shown so well that they were concerned about China, and would fight to save it, would not only benefit by land reform but exercise political power at the centre. Newspapers and journals circulated widely, in spite of the government censorship. *The People's Tribune* had begun publishing early in 1906. It was published in Tokyo. A very radical paper was published in Shanghai. Books circulated. Popular songs carried the message and broadcast the sentiments which undermined the Empire. People sang:

> All we want is to recover our land and they say it is rebellion! It is the shameless ones who would fight for them.
> We are only afraid of being like India, unable to defend our land; we are only afraid of being like Annam, of having no hope of reviving. We are only afraid of being like Poland, the Poles who drift about in an alien land; we are only afraid of being like the Jews, the Jews who are without a home!

and

> We Chinese have no part in this China of ours. This dynasty exists only in name! Being slaves of the foreigners, they force us common people to call them masters.

These popular songs were remembered many years later by Mr C. T. Liang, who wrote in his book, *The Chinese Revolution of 1911*,[4] of how popular the works of a man called Chen Tien-hua were. His books contained 'songs... full of nationalistic and revolutionary sentiments . . . written to the rhythm of popular tunes; they were propaganda works which went through many editions. Millions of copies were printed and circulated among the schools, the barracks and the countryside . . . That the Chinese soldiers and police refused to fight for the Manchus during the 1911 Revolution was due in part to these popular songs.'

Chen Tien-hua was one of the leading members of the United League. He was an impulsive man and, when the Chinese government got the Japanese authorities to make things difficult for Chinese students in Japan, Chen became so angry that he committed suicide. The contribution that writers of books and songs, like him, made to the work of building a base for a democratic China was substantial. Songs and music, slogans and posters, stories, even legends about great revolutionary leaders, and participation in action, all formed part of the popular culture of revolutionary struggle.

Sun had to leave Japan in 1907; it was not only the government in Peking but also that in Tokyo which wanted to obstruct the work of this dangerous man and his associates. The Japanese had restored collaboration with the Russians after defeating them in 1905. (The Tsarist regime in St Petersburg had more in common with Japan's rulers than with its rebellious subjects, some of whom had attempted a revolutionary uprising in 1905.) China was surrounded by an alliance of hostile powers. Sun had moved his own headquarters to Penang, in the British Straits Settlements, where the population, though certainly not the power, was predominantly Chinese. He set up a base of operations in French-ruled Indo-China; and himself led an attack on government forces in Yunnan province. He failed, and since he was recognized by Manchu spies, the French prohibited his future entry into their territory, even though some Frenchmen naturally had considerable sympathy for a republican movement.

Some time, probably in 1910, one of the highest imperial officials, Yuan Sih-kai, had secretly approached Sun. Yuan was a shrewd man and one of the ablest generals. He was a master of intrigue, and it was he who had betrayed the Emperor's plans at the time of the 'Hundred Days' Reform'. He appears to have realized that the days of the Manchus were numbered, and that popular support for Sun's radical policies were growing. A coup d'état by him, with Sun's public backing, would enable him to retain his powerful position. Sun, who had so far not been much interested in irrelevancies, naturally did not respond to Yuan's suggestion. He may have believed that there was something genuine in Yuan's profession of admiration for what he was doing, and in his offer to make it possible for him to enter China in safety. But that was no basis for a 'deal' with Yuan. 'Tell his Excellency I can wait. The Divine Right does not last for ever,' Sun told Yuan's messenger.

The temptation to say 'Yes' would have been great for any ordinary person. Sun was no longer a young man, and his life had been a hard one. When he was in North America early in 1911, he had a visitor who later described his impressions of Sun: 'He is very quiet and reserved in manner, and extremely moderate, cautious and thoughtful in speech. ... Dr Sun Yat-sen seems to be actuated by unselfish motives. ... I found him at a fourth-rate hotel, a kind of lodging house for working men, occupying a bare and miserable little room. His dress was modest and his luggage scanty.'[5] Yet Ellis Barker, who was Sun's visitor, was moved, as so many others were, by the sheer majesty of the man.

Sun was still in North America when he received a telegram sent from Hankow. His job was to carry on political agitation and raise money, for a good deal of work had yet to be done to build the United League into a strong and efficient organization. Too often in the past uprisings had failed and plans had been discovered by the government because of lack of arms, poor communications and bad transport facilities. Sun did not have his code-book with him, and could not decipher the message until several days had passed. He knew that after the failure of the

51

Canton uprising earlier that year Huang Hsing was still in China organizing another revolt. Ten days after he received it Sun read the telegram, and learnt of the plan for the revolutionaries to take Wuchang, in Hupeh province, where the local garrison was heavily infiltrated with members of the United League. Soon afterwards he read in the newspapers of the success at Wuchang. The revolutionaries had secured a base right in the heart of the country, in the central Yangtze region!

Sun was on the west coast, probably in the Canadian province of British Columbia. From Vancouver or San Francisco he could have reached Shanghai fairly quickly. But he did not rush back. He had no need to duplicate what Huang Hsing and other colleagues were doing. They could be left to take the initiative in the conduct of the revolutionary war while he attended to other urgent tasks. The imperialist powers with interests in China had to be persuaded to be neutral; and they had to be dissuaded from supplying funds which would enable the government to carry on a protracted struggle in which the revolutionaries, with no money (as Sun well knew) and inadequate weapons, would be at a disadvantage. Sun also knew the Japanese situation well enough to fear military intervention by the Japanese army or navy on behalf of the imperial government. In October 1911, while the chances of success across the Pacific seemed better than ever before in twenty-five years of revolutionary scheming, planning and action, the leader of the Tung-Meng Hui started on his journey to London. He hid his identity, so as to avoid the glare of personal publicity. This time the notorious bandit and troublemaker Sun Yat-sen disappeared for a while in a land in which he had on previous occasions travelled freely and openly.

Far away in China, among all the millions who were stirred to action by the revolution, was another peasant youth, who at the age of seventeen had read his first newspaper – one of the revolutionary papers – and had become an enthusiastic supporter of Sun. A rebel in his own family, he had left home against his father's wishes to go to school in Changsha, the capital of Hunan province, which was next to Hupeh. Now he decided that the time had come to fight for the Republic. He joined the revolutionary army, though he did not have to do any fighting, as Hunan fell easily into rebel hands. The youth, named Mao Tse-tung, could not have dreamt then that he would one day carry on the work that his hero Sun Yat-sen had begun.

NOTES

1. Li Chien-nung, op. cit., p. 179.
2. Cantlie and Jones, op. cit., pp. 64, 65.
3. *Memoirs of a Revolutionary*, pp. 14–15.
4. C. T. Liang, *The Chinese Revolution of 1911*, Jamaica, New York 1962, p. 12.
5. Quoted in Martin, p. 125.

6   The 1911 Revolution

There are accounts of the 1911 Revolution in China which make it out to have been due to an accident. A revolt by soldiers in one town leads to the collapse of the imperial forces. The republicans then take advantage of the situation and claim victory. This kind of caricature of Chinese politics has little relation to the facts. Revolutions do not happen like that. Even before the revolutionaries took Wuchang a struggle had been going on between the government and many groups of people over its railways policy. The corrupt Manchu nobles and their protégés, in their eagerness to enrich themselves, had provoked political agitation in the country. Consequently, foreign economic interests as well as the imperial court were seen as joint objects of opposition. The United League took advantage of the situation, to which their own political work had contributed.

There had for some time been competition among foreign business and financial interests for the monopoly of railway building in various parts of China. Control over the railways gave control – virtually extra-territorial rights – over a swathe of territory on either side of the railway. Such an acquisition was politically valuable; it was also highly profitable. Further, the foreign bankers played it in such a way that the money they provided for railway building was considered a loan, for the repayment of which they required guarantees. The intrigues of foreigners made the people increasingly anxious about the country's policy on railways. Japan and Russia had cemented their new friendship of 1907 by a joint policy for railway construction in Manchuria – a symbol of their collaboration in territorial expansion into north-eastern and north China.

In Hunan, Hupeh and Szechuan, railway building had been undertaken by the enterprise of the Chinese themselves. One might say that there was in the attempt to raise funds from merchants, labourers and peasants and invest them in economic ventures of this kind a development in the direction of Chinese capitalism, distinct from the compradore, or middleman activities, in which many Chinese in the commercial and industrial sector of the economy were engaged. In Szechuan, especially, the public interest in the railway was very great. The enthusiasts for the railway were, however, encroaching on areas which were vital to British and other foreign economic interests who had formed a consortium to raise funds. And Sheng Hsuan-huai, an embezzler of state funds who had, through intrigue, got the position of Minister of Posts in Peking, sold the Manchu court the idea that 'nationalization' of the railways being built with Chinese money would help divert some of the foreign funds of the consortium into the pockets of the Manchus. Accordingly, without any consultation or discussion with the people who owned the railways, an imperial decree was promulgated on 13 May 1911 nationalizing them. (Nationalizing meant ownership by the imperial family.) On 20 May the four-nation consortium (Britain, Germany, France and the United States) was formally given the contract to build the railway from Hankow to Szechuan and Hankow to Canton. The officials in Peking and the foreign diplomatic community at first made light of the uproar in Kwangtung, Hupeh, Hunan and, above all, in Szechuan, the most populous of the provinces. But the movement of protest grew.

Some of the terms of the agreement between Sheng and the foreign bankers had been kept secret. The Szechuan Railway Company and the public obviously could not be told how their railway was going to be shared out and how

55

much of their territory had been given away. But the confidence of the foreign consuls and the court was mistaken. The protests continued. There were strikes even in a political backwater like Szechuan. The continued agitation was providing ideal conditions for the work of the Tung-Meng Hui, and what had begun (surprisingly) as a struggle over the expropriation of the railway companies became rebellion. Troops had to be sent to Chengtu, the capital of Szechuan, but the shooting down of protesters did not bring about the submission of the province. From Wuchang (one of three cities on the Yangtze which together with Hankow and Hanyang make up Wuhan) more élite troops from the 'New Army' had to be sent to Szechuan. Wuchang, the city where the New Army was stationed, thus happened to be less strongly garrisoned than it usually was.[1]

An accidental bomb explosion in Hankow had made the police suspicious. They had warning that an uprising was being planned there when they discovered where the revolutionary headquarters was and raided it. The soldiers, who were members of the Tung-Meng Hui, had to act quickly, since lists of revolutionaries in the area had fallen into the hands of the police. It was a sergeant of an engineering battalion who gave the orders for the first attack, and men from the service corps and the cavalry joined them in an attack on the Governor-general's headquarters. The Governor-general and his commander panicked and fled. The fall of Wuchang precipitated the fall of Hanyang and Hankow, and thus put the revolutionaries suddenly in command of the strategically situated triple-city of Wuhan, and in control of Hupeh province. Twelve days after the Wuchang uprising the rebellion spread to Changsha, the capital of Hunan, which also fell easily. In a few weeks most of the provinces had gone over to the rebels.

The end of the Chinese Empire was one of the major events in world history. But it was not a spectacular event. It is not necessary in this book to go into the details of how the façade of the old imperial China crumbled. The revolution was a much more protracted and complex event and process than the final series of blows which knocked down the hollow shell of the building. Many of the things which had kept the Manchus in power – the apathy of the people, the lack of a national identity, the dominance of traditional ways of thinking and doing things, the feeling of helplessness and so on – had been changed, wholly or partly, by revolutionary activity.

There were difficulties greater than the strength of the imperial regime. Foreign intervention was a real danger. When Sun arrived in London he found a telegram waiting for him, asking him to be President of the new Republic of China. Sun had decided, as he confided to his friends the Cantlies, that he would accept the post provisionally, if no one else could be found. The fact that matters of this nature – who was to be President? Who was to be Commander-in-chief? What would new government be like? – became urgent, and tended to be all-absorbing, was a danger to the revolution as Sun had conceived it. These matters were not unimportant; they had to be dealt with properly if the allegiance of the whole nation was to be given to the new government; it was also necessary to attend to them as quickly as possible in order to minimize another difficulty, or danger – that of foreign intervention. But the new Republic, if it was going to be one in which citizens of equal status freely chose the President and the parliament, had yet to complete the revolution by transforming the livelihood of the people. For Sun, journeying towards the China in the throes of a revolution for which he above all others was responsible, the overthrow of the Ching dynasty had long ago ceased to be the main objective of the Tung-Meng Hui. The other leaders of the revolution – Huang Hsing, Hu Han-min, Sung Chiao-jen and others – could well handle the military phase of the struggle, but they were not agreed among themselves and with Sun about the poli-

57

tical and economic tasks which had to be accomplished before their work could be considered successful.

The second danger arose from the fact that foreign organizations established in China, and foreign governments most of which were stronger militarily and economically than any Chinese government could be for some time, were entangled in China's affairs. They had on many previous occasions intervened militarily in China. They had so little respect for any civilized principles of international relations – which would have demanded respect for the sovereignty of the Chinese over their land – that they could despatch their armies and navies to prevent the overthrow of the regime; it was one which foreigners found so compliant that only the mutual jealousies, intrigues and treacheries of the competing imperialist powers had preserved China. Never averse to occupying territory they coveted, some of these imperialist powers, especially near neighbours like Japan and Russia, could make use of a civil war to start partitioning China. The attainment of one of the Tung-Meng Hui's main aims – revolutionary nationalism – would be made impossible if China was broken up.

In later years much effort went into attempts to suggest that Sun played an insignificant role in the 1911 Revolution. The reasons for this campaign of denigration are important, and must be considered later. On his arrival in London in the autumn of 1911 Sun was by no means a person to be treated lightly. Here was a man who had done what he had set out to do. Whether or not people liked what he had done in bringing about a major uprising in China, there were serious risks in not dealing with the man who was reported to have been nominated President of the new Chinese Republic. The future of the foreign businesses in China might depend on their governments and principals (in the metropolitan countries) not antagonizing the revolutionaries. Sun was therefore treated as a person who spoke and negotiated with some authority when he dealt with the British government and the banking consortium whose activities had roused the Szechuanese and their neighbours to rebellion. He got the loan to the imperial government stopped. He also persuaded the British government to take action 'to prevent Japan from helping the dynasty'. There was also the British government's ban on his entry into British territory; this the future President of China persuaded the government in London to revoke, so that he could return home more easily. Sun tried to get the banking consortium to make available a loan to the revolutionary government, but this was a matter on which the bankers would not commit themselves. Before leaving Europe for China. Sun also made a call on Clemenceau, the French Prime Minister. He also met representatives of the French opposition parties.

The revolutionary leader was no longer travelling secretly and in disguise. There was a great reception for him in Penang. and again in Hong Kong. The long journey by sea was, by the standards of our day, very slow; it was certainly too slow to match the speed of developments in China. By the time he reached Shanghai, on 24 December, his absence had made itself felt in the revolutionary party. The difficult situation that existed, with all its complications, was by no means as bad as that in which the Manchus found themselves. For the imperial authority remained only in Chihli, Shantung and Hunan provinces, in addition to the Manchurian provinces of the north-east, whereas the revolutionaries held fourteen provinces; and the suspension of aid by the consortium had forced the dowager empress to sell an enormous part of the dynasty's hoard of gold in order to raise funds for the defeat of the revolution. Nevertheless, the revolutionary ranks were thoroughly disorganized, and the sudden accession to their ranks of all sorts of groups which had jumped on to the successful revolutionary bandwagon had created the kind of confusion in which important decisions had been arrived at with little care for future consequences. Sun Yat-sen, on his arrival, had to discover in greater detail what the situation was, and what the consequences might be of the decisions his politically naïve and divided colleagues had made. Having been elected Provisional President of the Republic by sixteen out of the seventeen representatives of the provinces, he assumed office on 1 January 1912, the inauguration day of the Republic. He presented his list of appointments to the cabinet of ministers, which the representatives approved. Huang Hsing was included as Minister of the Army, and the Minister of Education was a member of the Tung-Meng Hui named Tsai Yuan-pei.

'Thus thirty years passed as one day,' Sun wrote in his memoirs, 'and only after their completion did I achieve my principal aim, the aim of my life – the creation of the Chinese Republic.'[2] On 5 January Sun and his Foreign Minister issued a 'Manifesto to all friendly nations from the Republic of China'. It began, in tones characteristic of manifestoes in general:

Greeting. The hitherto irremediable suppression of the individual qualities and national aspirations of the people having arrested the intellectual, the moral, and the material development of China, the aid of revolution has been invoked to extirpate the primary cause, and we now proclaim the resultant overthrow of the despotic sway wielded by the Manchu Dynasty and the establishment of a Republic. . . .

It went on in less high-sounding terms to explain to the 'free people of the world' the reasons for the revolution, pointing out that the backwardness, isolation and humiliation of the Chinese people was a phenomenon of the Manchu period, not of earlier periods of Chinese history. The Manchus 'levied irregular and unwholesome taxes upon us without our consent, have restricted foreign trade to Treaty Ports, placed like embargoes upon merchandise in transit, and obstructed internal commerce. They have retarded the creation of industrial enterprises, rendered impossible the development of natural resources . . .' and been guilty of tyranny, corruption and other evils.

It went on to say:

> It will be our constant aim and firm endeavour to build upon a stable and enduring foundation a national structure compatible with the potentialities of our long-neglected country.
>
> We will strive to elevate our people; secure them in peace, and legislate for their prosperity.
>
> To those Manchus who abide peacefully within the limits of our jurisdiction we will accord equality and give protection.
>
> We will remodel our laws; revise our civil, criminal, commercial and mining codes; reform our finances; abolish restrictions to trade and commerce, and ensure religious toleration.
>
> The cultivation of better relations with foreign peoples and governments will ever be before us. It is our earnest hope that the foreign nations who have been steadfast in sympathy will bind more firmly the bonds of friendship, that they will bear in patience with us in the period of trial confronting us in our reconstructive work, and that they will aid us in the consummation of the far-reaching plans which we are now about to undertake, and which they have been so long and so vainly urging upon the people of this our country.
>
> With this message of peace and goodwill the Republic of China cherishes the hope of being admitted into the family of nations, not merely to share their rights and privileges but also to cooperate with them in the great and noble task called for in the upbuilding of the civilization of the world.

On 15 February President Sun with his entourage paid a ceremonial visit to the mausoleum of the first Emperor of the Ming dynasty, which was established in the fourteenth century after the defeat and overthrow of the Mongol Yuan dynasty. The ceremony was an elaborate one, involving an invocation to the spirit of the last Chinese who had liberated the country from rule by a half-foreign dynasty, and in its traditional gesture and in the emotion it aroused in the masses it sought to give the new, non-monarchical Republic continuity with the old institutions. The ceremony just outside Nanking appears to have moved the people very deeply. Some foreign comments, written in the characteristically contemptuous tones in which China and the Chinese were ridiculed, did not understand what the ceremony meant.

If the story of Sun Yat-sen, the revolutionary whose work transformed the 2000-year-old Chinese Empire into a republic, had ended here, we could attempt an appraisal of his achievement. The peasant boy who had been revolted by the servility and superstition which had helped the continuance of Manchu rule had been chosen the leader of a new China! A new era had begun in Chinese history! Now that the Tung-Meng Hui was the ruling party, the policies of equalization of land ownership, industrialization, democratic government and so on which had been Sun's ideals could be translated into policies and programmes! Revolutions, however, do not happen in this way. The story we are telling is not that of Sun Yat-sen as a private person. Sun Yat-sen the revolutionary and statesman was to discover, as soon as the Manchus had been repudiated by the people, that it was premature to write his memoirs. In the thirteen years of life left to him after the inauguration of the Republic of China, Sun was to be as busy as he had ever been; he was to face dangers of a kind he never experienced when he was being hunted by the agents of the imperial government.

People who have achieved great things in the prime of their lives do not always enhance their reputations in later life. On the contrary, great leaders not infrequently find themselves in circumstances which show up inadequacies and flaws, and make misjudgments which bring on them disgrace or opprobrium. We are not thinking here merely of the tendency for people to get corrupted by fame, prestige or power which they have been accorded because of their achievements; and we are not thinking at all of the decline which accompanies senility. What Sun in his middle forties was challenged by was not power, prestige or fading mental powers, but something else which we shall not attempt to define in the abstract. What it was the story of his record as a statesman and revolutionary after 1912 will reveal.

This is an appropriate moment to recall the impression that Sun made on Ellis Barker early in 1911. Barker, it will be remembered, had called on Sun while he was in British Columbia, trying to win support among Chinese emigrants. He relates how after he had been talking to Sun late into the night at his (Barker's) hotel, he was anxious about Sun's safety during his walk back to his own hotel. Sun did not want Barker to trouble to walk with him. Barker remonstrated that with a price of £100,000 on his head he was in danger; if he did not think of himself, he should at least spare himself for his cause and his country. To this Sun had replied: 'If they had killed me some years ago, it would have been a pity for the cause; I was indispensable then. Now my life does not matter. Our organization is complete. There are plenty of Chinaman to take my place. It does not matter if they kill me.' Barker's comment on this episode was: 'Simple, unaffected and modest, Dr Sun Yat-sen gives one the impression of a really great man in the fullest sense of the word. It is ridiculous to compare him with Benjamin Franklin and with Garibaldi, for he stands by himself, and is likely to be classed in history among the world's greatest men. . . . No greater task has ever been attempted than that of reforming the oldest and the most conservative State the world has seen, and of converting it into a republic. The reform of Japan is but a small thing compared with the recreation of China.'[3]

Such admiration as this was not unjustified. Dr Cantlie, one of the few Europeans who know Sun well, spoke for many when he expressed admiration and wonder at Sun's selflessness and incorruptibility, and provides the obvious explanation for the campaigns to belittle and ridicule Sun's achievements. Sun was undoubtedly sincere in his making the offer of the presidency to Yuan, and in his support for Yuan in 1912. But it is not as an act of personal morality that we must judge each of the things Sun did. To speak in terms of the *personal* sacrifice in renouncing power and office is to appraise a revolutionary and a statesman totally outside the context of political practice and of social and political forces. Sun's actions were political ones. There is no intrinsic virtue in the renunciation of political authority. Sun announced his resignation on 12 February, and formally handed over the authority of the President of the Chinese Republic to one of the officials of the Manchu dynasty, Yuan Shih-kai. If he was doing it *because he believed it was good to renounce power* he was a foolish man, a bad revolutionary and the source of the disasters which resulted from Yuan's assumption of the presidency.

We need, in order to understand Sun's career after China's repudiation of the Manchus, to know what freedom of action the revolutionaries had. What were the options? What were the hard and unpleasant necessities forced on the revolutionaries by the situation within China and by China's position in the international order of the day. We have, in other words, to be very specific about the political situation in China from 1912 until Sun's death in 1925. Sun knew a great deal about China as a whole – perhaps more than anyone else at that time. Until he found himself leader of a victorious revolutionary party he did not have to make decisions on which the whole future of China might depend. It is his policies and decisions by which he must be judged.

NOTES

1. Accounts of these events are to be found in Han Suyin's colourful *The Crippled Tree*, Jonathan Cape 1965, pp. 220–68 and Wu Yu-chang, *The Revolution of 1911*, Peking 1964.

2. *Memoirs of a Revolutionary*, p. 20.

3. Martin, op. cit., p. 125.

7   The Revolution Betrayed

In the sixteen years since Sun Yat-sen's first revolutionary attempt the efforts of the conservatives and of the constitutional reformers had not prevented republican ideas from taking hold in various parts of China. Some people, especially the returned students who had had close contact with Sun in Japan or Europe, had a fairly clear understanding of the radical changes through which China would have to go in order to become a modern, educated democracy, instead of continuing to be a benighted, backward despotism. Others had vaguer notions of what kind of China the United League (Tung-Meng Hui) was leading them towards. There were a variety of local organizations which adopted the general aim of the revolutionaries – that of overthrowing the ruling dynasty and changing the nature of the regime. There were members of various secret societies who collaborated with the revolutionaries against the common enemy, though they did not intend to help create a democratic republic. Because the opponents of the regime and their foreign backers had to work underground and avoid turning against one another, political questions were not pressed too hard. In any case, opportunities for nationwide discussions hardly existed, except when people went abroad or circulated revolutionary literature; there were yet no national universities in which free discussion could take place, not even the rather limited opportunities provided by parliaments in the capitalist countries; there were no peasant unions, trade unions or national associations of those belonging to modern professions. Any unified conception of revolutionary strategy could hardly exist among the

C

people who had to fight for the creation of a republic.

A protracted struggle would have helped people to learn their politics in the course of revolutionary practice. The waverers and the opportunists would then have been identified more easily, and the masses would have had increasing opportunities for active leadership in the revolutionary struggle. A revolution cannot transcend the material conditions in which it takes place. The people, with their immense capacity for change and creativity, are the main material factor in a revolution. But what they could have done was limited by the miserable state of communications within the country: places not connected by water were separated by the absence of roads, railways, radio and telephone communication and by vast distances. The very fact that the struggle was against Manchu princes and nobles – a minority people from the extreme north-east – rather than against a whole class of aristocrats or lords to be found in every province, affected the nature of the action that the people took. Landlords, rich merchants, even senior officials and officers who were not Manchu, could join with the truly oppressed – the poor peasants, the coolies, artisans who had been ruined, ordinary soldiers, women and those proscribed for their patriotism – in fighting for the end of the old order. And with the advantages they had of better education and freedom from the necessity of toil, they could bid for leadership of provincial and even the national revolutionary administrations.

The rebellions in Szechuan and Hupeh provinces had very rapidly been followed by others in Hunan, Shensi, Shansi, Kiangsi, Kiangsu, Kweichow, Chekiang, Anhwei, Kwangtung and Fukien. The members of the Tung-Meng Hui who were in the government's New Army and in the secret societies had mobilized important forces. Under good commanders who knew how to conduct revolutionary warfare, the republican forces could have withstood attempts by the crack troops from Peking to win China back to the conservatives. To do that they would have to submit to a unified command. It did not exist. The landlords, rich peasants and merchants who flocked to join the rebels had no stomach for prolonged fighting, and they must have realized the consequences for them of a protracted struggle. One of the possible consequences would be the increasing radicalization of the leadership. The other was the risk of foreign intervention. Neither was desirable, from their point of view, and they preferred to admit reactionary nationalists and even agents of the Manchus to a share in power rather than complete the revolution.

Sun, having trusted his colleagues to take initiatives and make decisions in his absence, had to accept what had been decided. For him the danger of foreign intervention must have been very real. The radicalization of the movement was what he had worked all his life to accomplish, The programme of the Tung-Meng Hui had raised great hopes. Women had joined the revolutionary army and fought for a China in which they would be free from the oppression they had suffered. The peasants and other labourers did not leave it to the landlords to take control of events. As a participant in the revolution later related: 'Fierce struggles against the feudal system were waged by the peasants. In Kiangsu, Kwangtung and Hunan, for instance, many peasants, having managed to arm themselves, fought against feudal oppression and meted out punishment to the local despots and bad gentry. Peasant uprisings of different magnitudes broke out in various other provinces. The one which broke out in Szechuan was on a particular [sic] big scale. With the exception of the Taiping Heavenly Kingdom no peasant uprising in modern Chinese history compares with it.'[1] Sun must have been delighted that the people had risen up in this way. Why then did he not oppose the political alliances and compromises which betrayed the revolution?

The danger of foreign intervention needs to be considered.

Britain had agreed to remain neutral in the conflict between the Manchus and the revolutionaries. The Japanese were caught by surprise when the revolution began, and different groups among them worked on different lines; they thus failed to exploit the revolutionary war to their advantage. It was Japanese intervention that Sun had feared most, and with good reason. When the Wuchang Uprising took place Japan had apparently offered to put it down, but the court in Peking refused the offer. On 15 October the Japanese government had informed the US government that it had been requested to put down the rebellion, but would not intervene unless the revolution spread to theManchurian provinces, in which case they would send 20,000 troops into Peking. Early in December the Japanese proposed to intervene if the hostilities between north and south continued. And again on 18 December the Japanese proposed to the Americans that a nominal Manchu regime should be established under the joint guarantee of the powers.[2] They also intrigued to detach the far northern and north-eastern provinces from China with the help of Manchu and Mongolian princes. Added to this danger of what foreign powers might do was that of a partition of the country. We know from the experience of other nations how deadly it is for any country to allow a situation to develop which enables a foreign power to establish a puppet regime on any part of its territory. The Chinese, having been concerned about the danger of China's being broken up by foreign powers, would not have wanted to risk that happening as a result of prolonged civil war.

In joining with his colleagues in trying to win over Peking's Prime Minister, General Yuan Shih-kai, Sun was trying to avoid war between North China (still under Manchu rule) and South China, now a republic. By offering to resign in favour of Yuan, who would become President of the Republic, Sun was, in a sense, offering the unprincipled Yuan a bribe. This is a harsh way of describing the negotiations with Yuan which dragged on till February 1912. Sun was not after office or wealth; but continued leadership of the revolutionary movement was something he owed all his followers who still had to enjoy the political and economic benefits of the observance of the Three Principles, and particularly that which involved equalization of landownership.

Unless the Manchu princes and nobles, who had held power, accepted the establishment of the Republic, and accepted the republican terms on which they could be allowed to live in peace, the fighting would have to go on. Yuan's intrigues were not helping the situation. In mid-January the Nanking government demanded from Yuan that the Manchu Emperor should formally abdicate and give up all the powers he claimed; that he (the Emperor) should undertake not to interfere at all in the organization of the provisional government; that the capital be in Nanking and that President Sun's resignation should come only after the provisional government had been recognized by all the powers, the domestic reform had been achieved, and peace well established; that Yuan Shih-kai should not interfere in any matters of the provisional government before the resignation of President Sun.

The tiresome negotiations did not end when the Manchus finally gave in. For the abdication announcement drawn up for the Emperor violated the conditions laid down by the revolutionaries; he was made to speak as though *he* gave Yuan authority. Nevertheless, the senate of the provisional government, acting on Sun's recommendation, nominated Yuan to succeed Sun as President. Yuan then refused to move to Nanking. And they gave in to him. Yuan thus got away with his refusal to submit to the authority of the revolutionary government. He had the support of the chiefs of his army – the Peiyang military clique, as they came to be called. And he had the support of the foreign diplomats, who opposed the move of the Chinese capital to Nanking.

Sun insisted on agreements being honoured, but he found that he was isolated; Yuan had resorted to his usual trickery, including the staging of an army riot in Peking, and the delegation from Nanking yielded to him. Sun, still believing that Yuan would honour his oath, formally handed over the presidency to Yuan on 1 April 1912, and became a private citizen. On 5 April the senate moved the capital back to the imperial city, Peking, where Yuan's military forces were based.

Sun was right to withdraw from the presidency when he realized that leading party members did not intend to honour their revolutionary pledges. He was right to argue that he did not support 'substitution of new bureaucrats for old ones'. But should he have handed over to a man like Yuan a power which the revolutionaries alone had the right to dispose of? Yuan was, no doubt, highly favoured by the foreigners and the conservatives. That was hardly a recommendation. Huang Hsing, Sung Chiao-jen, Hu Han-min and other colleagues were limited in their outlook, but they had fought courageously for the establishment of the Republic. They were more honourable men than Yuan was known to be at the time of the handing over of power. Sun had blundered, as he was to realize later on. The revolutionary hope which in 1895 led him to take on the power of the Chinese Empire was weak when he contemplated the threats of the Japanese imperialists and betrayal by his colleagues. He was getting isolated from the Chinese people. The events of the next few years were to make this fact clear, and to challenge him to a renewal of his revolutionary commitment to the poor and oppressed.

To be fair to Sun we must accept his plea that if the revolutionary programme was not to be carried out the Chinese people would only be 'exchanging one tyrant for another'! But he could hardly have hoped to turn Yuan into the revolutionary President his colleagues had not allowed him to be. He appears to have lost confidence in his own powers of leadership. That he sensed his failure we can gather from what he wrote about the period immediately following the 1911 Revolution:

> When the Republic was first established in 1912, I strongly urged putting the 'programme of revolution' into effect, in order to achieve the goal of revolutionary reconstruction and the application of the Three Principles of the People. But most of our party members were hesitant, and thought it could not be done. Although I repeatedly explained and argued, it was all to no avail. They all held that my revolutionary ideals were too high. . . . Alas, were my ideals too high? Was it not rather that the knowledge of our party members was too low? Therefore I could not help becoming discouraged and disappointed. . . . Since there was no revolutionary reconstruction, what use would there be for a revolutionary President? That is why I, desiring to retire after the establishment of the Nanking Government, continued the armistice and renewed peace negotiations. . . .[3]

Retirement was no solution. A quick survey of the events following Yuan's assumption of power in China will tell us what had gone wrong. The Tung-Meng Hui, which had been an underground organization, became an open political party late in 1911. In August 1912 Sung Chiao-jen, who had been one of the people elected to the leadership of the Tung-Meng Hui when it was founded in 1905, took the lead in reorganizing it. It was combined with a small group called the United Republican Party to become the Kuomintang, or Nationalist Party. Sung was an able and ambitious man, and in the elections held early in 1913 to the new house of representatives of the Republic, the Kuomintang won more seats than any other party. Party membership was regarded somewhat loosely in China, since a man might belong to more than one party at the same time. Sung, however, was clearly in a position to claim that he should be made Prime Minister.

Yuan had already had trouble with the first Prime Minister he had to work with. Although he was a man whom Yuan had wanted, he was very strict in his dealings with the President, and did not allow him to act arbitrarily.

Much to the fury of the consortium of imperialist bankers (from Britain, the United States, Germany, France, Japan and Russia) he tried to take steps to break their domination of China's financial affairs. He opposed Yuan on appointments, and the President had to get the army chiefs to threaten violent action if the government acted independently. The Prime Minister would not tolerate that, and resigned, and with him other members of the cabinet who belonged to the Tung-Meng Hui. Yuan then got his warlord friends to threaten to murder the members of the senate if they did not do as he wanted. With the military power at his disposal, Yuan seized absolute power, leaving the senate, which in any case had ceased to stand for any revolutionary principles, to function merely as a rubber stamp. He wanted to hurry through arrangements for a loan from the consortium. Acceptance of the terms of the loan would have been unfavourable to the rising capitalist forces in China who were willing to tolerate Yuan's despotic ways on other matters. There was a controversy which the foreign governments found embarrassing. It was round about this time that the elections for the first parliament were held, and the Kuomintang emerged as the majority party.

The Kuomintang had already taken a tough position with Yuan, contrary to Sun's advice. Sun had wanted his party to continue work among the people, and not to provoke a confrontation with Yuan. He probably felt that since his former associates had renounced the 'goal of revolutionary reconstruction', they would be fighting merely for power. Sun had been due to pay a visit to Japan – what was virtually a state visit, though he was no longer President – in December 1912. The visit was postponed, and he arrived in Japan on 13 February, to remain there till 22 March. His thoughts had turned a great deal to the problems of modernization in China, and he did not appear to be involved in party politics. The policy that Sung Chiao-jen advocated, a policy which would involve curbing the President's powers, could not have been entirely to Sun's liking. But the assassination of Sung brought Sun Yat-sen back into active politics.

The leader of the Kuomintang was shot and killed in Shanghai as he was going to catch a train. The assassin and his accomplice were discovered and arrested. They had documents on them which implicated the Prime Minister and Yuan Shih-kai himself in the assassination plot. The official inquiry was a thorough one, and on 26 April its conclusions were published, giving details of the evidence. It was clear that the Prime Minister, a protégé of Yuan, had been planning the assassination for some months, and that Yuan had known about it. The scandal did not end there. The assassin was not punished. But some time later, when he 'talked', he was assassinated. The Prime Minister whose order he had carried out was now governor of Chihli, and started investigating his death; *he* was then murdered. To such a sordid state Sun's successor had reduced the Chinese Republic.

The Chinese historian, Li Chien-nung, writes:

> Yuan's motive in taking Sung's life was, very likely, his recognition that since the Kuomintang had been successful in getting votes in the parliament, Sung would make use of this majority to compel Yuan to reorganize the cabinet; to destroy the Kuomintang it was necessary to destroy its leaders first. There were, however, many other leaders. Why was Sung alone assassinated: because Yuan knew that Sun Yat-sen at that time had no intention of antagonizing him, Huang was too naïve and honest, while a few others with rank equal to Sung in the party had either been bribed by Yuan or did not wish to draw unfavourable attention to themselves.'[4]

Li relates how Yuan had made it a regular practice to bribe Kuomintang members. He had sent Sung, too, a cheque book for drawing on a particular bank account. Sung, having as a matter of courtesy drawn a small amount, had returned the cheque book to the President!

After Yuan's part in the murder of Sung was proved, Sun Yat-sen was at last stirred into action. His party was weak, demoralized and confused. He decided that the best way to bring Yuan to see reason would be to get foreign governments and agencies to respect constitutional processes in China. Sun had been generous and idealistic in his dealings with Yuan, and he expected foreign bankers to respond to an appeal for decency. On the very day that the facts about the Sung assassination were published, 26 April, the consortium had signed the constitutionally invalid agreement for the 'Reorganization Loan' with Yuan. £25,000,000 was involved and the terms resulted in further diminution of China's sovereignty. Sun drafted a telegram to be sent overseas for publication. One of Yuan's missionary supporters, a Dr Timothy Richard, visited Sun and tried to dissuade him from sending it. Sun refused. Part of his telegram said:

... From date of birth of Republic I have striven for unity, peace, concord and prosperity. I recommended Yuan Shih-kai for presidency because there appeared reasons for believing that by doing so unification of nation and dawn of era of peace and prosperity would thereby be hastened. Ever since then I have done all I could to evolve peace, order and government out of chaos created by revolution. I earnestly desire to preserve peace throughout Republic, but my efforts will be rendered ineffective if financiers will supply Peking government with money that would and probably will be used in waging war against people. If country is plunged into war at this juncture it will inevitably inflict terrible misery and suffering upon people who are just beginning to recover from dislocation of trade and losses of various kinds caused by revolution. For establishment of Republic they have sacrificed much and are now determined to preserve it at all costs. If people are now forced into life and death struggle for preservation of Republic not only will it entail terrible suffering to masses but inevitably and adversely affect all foreign interests in China. If Peking government is kept without funds there is prospect of compromise between it and people being effected, while immediate effect of liberal supply of money will probably be precipitation of terrible and disastrous conflict. In name and for sake of humanity which civilization holds sacred I therefore appeal to you to exert your influence with view to preventing bankers from providing Peking government with funds which at this juncture will assuredly be utilized as sinews of war. . . .[5]

Yuan Shih-kai had violated the Chinese constitution and used force in order to allow foreign capitalist powers to get a firmer hold of China's economy than they had before; he had also undertaken to respect the unequal treaties which Sun and his colleagues were critical of. Yuan was the kind of person who got a good press in the West; *The Times* in particular helped him by ridiculing and slandering Sun. And he had missionary friends, chief among them Dr Goodnow, who advised and helped him in other ways. The very thing which Sun declared the Chinese people feared was what the consortium and the admirers of Yuan wanted: a man who was the puppet of foreign interests and a dictator in regard to the Chinese people. As could have been expected, Sun's appeal was disregarded, and Yuan got his loan.

Yuan now moved for a showdown with the remaining opposition. The revolution could be saved only by the removal of Yuan, for Sun's appeal to him to resign did not, naturally, have any effect, But could Yuan be overthrown? The enthusiasm and vigour of 1911 had faded. On 12 July 1913 the 'Second Revolution' began, but it ended in defeat. The mass of the people did not rise up in support. Yuan had enough money to bribe people he did not want to fight, and he used it. The opposition to him was badly organized and collapsed very quickly. Sun, Huang Hsing and other leaders had to flee. Central China came under the rule of the Peiyang military clique. Yuan dispensed with the constitution and with parliament and ruled with the help of office-seekers and hangers-on. It was no problem for him eventually to have himself 'invited' to become Emperor.

It must have been deeply disappointing to Sun that the people – those who had originally given him inspiration and for whom he had laboured – did not rally to the support of those who dared to resist the new tyranny of Yuan and the warlords. It made sense for the gentry (who by tradition had a great deal of power and influence locally) to want to compromise with Yuan rather than to follow a man with revolutionary aims. But, as we must see in more detail later, the dangers which had threatened China as a whole had not been lessened by the compromise made with Yuan in 1911–12. If the newly-rising class of rich peasants and manufacturers had any loyalties to the nation they should have joined in the opposition to Yuan. The indifference of the poorer peasants and the labouring masses in the cities and towns was more serious. It has sometimes been explained by historians that they were tired of fighting and wanted peace. This kind of explanation ignores the fact that people who are oppressed and are steadily getting poorer do not have peace. The Chinese masses had several times in the past shown a much greater concern for their country than had their rulers. The reasons why they did not respond now were not simple, but they were good ones. After the defeat of the Manchus, some of the leading members of the Kuomintang (and the Tung-Meng Hui just before) had been arrogant and self-seeking; they had made use of popular support for the 1911 Revolution in order to advance the material interests of their own cliques and their own personal ambitions. Moreover, the increasing poverty in the villages was partly caused by their greed.

There was a more profound reason. The revolutionary leaders had taken a cynical view of the principles on which the revolutionary movement had been built. Sun had fought against this, but the Kuomintang, which was the main force opposing Yuan, had little claims on the trust and loyalty of the people. Sung Chiao-jen had found it politic, when he campaigned for votes, to get rid of one of the main aims of the revolution: equalization of land-ownership. Earlier, the women who had fought in the revolutionary war had their armed units disbanded. On 19 March 1912 a women's demonstration protesting against the constitution tried to force its way into the parliament building; they broke windows and caused some trouble, but they were unable to reverse the betrayal by the new government of the understanding that discrimination against women would be ended. The Kuomintang first included in its platform equality between men and women, but abandoned this in order to win votes.

Sun was an exile at the end of 1913. But it was not his personal plight but that of millions of Chinese who were betrayed and frustrated that must make us critical of his leadership.

NOTES

1. Wu Yu-chang, op. cit., p. 131.
2. Liang, op. cit., p. 44.
3. Quoted in Ssu-yu Teng and John K. Fairbank, *China's Response to the West*, CUP 1954, p. 261.
4. Li Chien-nung, op. cit., p. 288.
5. Martin, op. cit., p. 162.

8 The Problem of the International Order

Sun Yat-sen's life was an untidy one, as the lives of most people are. It does not appear that Sun ever realized how important a man he was. It may not have entered his head to reflect on what he had achieved by the time he resigned his position of Provisional President of the Chinese Republic, in order to work for his country at a more humble level of authority. The revolution had released long-pent-up forces within China which the counter-revolutionary efforts of the imperialist powers and of the conservatives could never again bottle up. The revolutionary struggle against the imperial Manchu-dominated order had slowly destroyed it and made its complete collapse inevitable. All revolutions, it would be correct to say, begin only when the revolutionaries have the power to transform and to create. What the Chinese people, in spite of Yuan and the warlords, did in the decade and a half following the inauguration of the Republic, is partly to the credit of Sun Yat-sen. If we have been critical of some of Sun's decisions, and of the decisions of some of the men Sun had as his colleagues, and if we saw the darker side of Chinese politics during 1911–13 in the last chapter, we can appreciate the fact that Sun himself looked critically at his performance of his great task. Sun was yet to discover that he had done more than anyone else to give a new lease of life to a great civilization and to a great people.

What went on in China in the first fifteen years of the new era is part of the life story of Sun. We shall have to look at it. The revolutionary ferment transformed China so much that the China of the 'twenties was a different land from the China of the years before the First World War. It could be interesting to take a look at the way the emergence of the Chinese Republic was regarded outside China, and the effect of the policies of foreign governments and industrial and financial organizations on Chinese politics. We have already made some references to international interest in Chinese affairs and the support given to Yuan. We have not asked why foreigners continued to create such great difficulties for the Chinese in the twentieth century. Why did they want Yuan and the warlords to triumph over their opponents? Why were they hostile to the revolutionaries?

The uprisings of 1911 and the struggle to establish a properly constitutional form of republican government took place at a time when China's territorial integrity was seriously threatened. We have already noticed how much Sun and his colleagues in 1911 feared that prolonged war between the revolutionary and the Manchu forces might result in the loss of parts of China to foreign powers. We have not considered how reasonable their fears were. Europeans and North Americans have vague feelings of guilt about the expansionist and imperialist policies practised in the past and still practised by their governments and business companies. But, understandably, they often cannot credit the peoples of the Third World with good sense and realism in fighting to recover and protect their homelands. Moreover, imperialism, and the racialism of the world order created in the imperialist period, have often been justified on the grounds of philanthropy and the 'missionary imperative'. There have therefore been obstacles to any understanding of events in China in Sun's lifetime and after. Today, sixty years after the 1911 Revolution, China is still, as it was then, the centre of the struggle against the expansionist policies and racial pretensions of the West; those who want to crush armed opposition to imperialism find China the main enemy. It is not easy for some of us to read about earlier events without feeling some of the hostile emotions which are aroused when the 'rights' and 'freedoms' of the imperialist powers are challenged, and when the western presence in Third World countries is described as aggression.

For the Chinese who were patriotic and concerned, too, about social justice and economic development, imperialist aggression was something very tangible, and indeed painfully so. Parts of Chinese territory had already been lost to neighbours. Some parts were colonies; some were 'leased'. All had been taken by foreigners by violent means. Then there were the 'concessions' and the 'settlements'. There were British concessions in Canton, Hankow, Tientsin and three other cities; there were French concessions in Shanghai, Hankow, Tientsin and Canton; the Japanese had concessions in Tientsin and three other cities; there were Russian, German, Belgian, Italian and Austrian concessions. There was the vast International Settlement in Shanghai. Foreigners traded freely in these alien territories; they administered their own form of justice, levied taxes, maintained police or military forces. The Legation Quarter in Peking had a privileged status well beyond that of mere diplomatic immunity.

Foreigners who carried on trade and other activities or merely travelled in other parts of China were not subject to the jurisdiction of Chinese courts. Foreign authorities controlled the national postal service. Foreign governments had imposed on Chinese governments an absolute limit on the rate of customs duty as early as 1842, and the customs service was effectively under foreign control, the revenue going into foreign-owned banks operating in China. Foreign authorities decided what portion of this revenue should be used to pay the various dues of the Chinese government. These dues were considerable, since the demand for 'indemnities' had become a habit with the foreigners

80

in power; there was interest to be extracted for the loans raised to pay indemnities and other loans. The diplomatic corps in Peking then decided if and how what was left over should be allocated to the Chinese government. After Yuan's 'reorganization loan' of 1913 the consortium powers took control of the revenue from the salt tax. The 'debt' which was the excuse for the assertion of foreign administrative control over the finances of the Chinese government had nothing whatever to do with the economic development of China, except in a negative way; that is, the money borrowed had not been used for purposes of China's development. The revenue collected was of value to the banks. And it was left to the foreign governments or their agencies to decide which person or group in the country was to receive the 'Chinese' share of the revenue. That share could be used, and was used, to buy what the foreign powers wanted in the way of good behaviour.

It is estimated that property owned by foreign companies in China just before the First World War was valued at over one-and-a-half billion dollars. In addition, there were different areas of China over which one power or another exercised a kind of suzerainty; these were 'spheres of influence'. Foreigners had the freedom and the right in the existing situation to establish institutions like schools, hospitals and universities, in furtherance of their own interests and policies. They controlled the discipline and decided the theology of churches to which Chinese belonged. They published their own newspapers, ran radio stations and had military and naval bases in China.

The Revolution of 1911 had not altered this situation. It took place only within the area of sovereignty left to the Chinese by the dominant imperialist powers – a sovereignty severely limited geographically, economically, administratively, politically and culturally. China was, as Sun was to say, the colony not of one but of all; or, to put it in more contemporary terms, she was a semi-colony of a United Nations of capitalist powers. For the Chinese who wanted to realize the revolutionary aims embodied in Sun's Three Principles an appraisal of imperialism was unavoidable. Nothing like what obtained in China was to be found as a whole anywhere else in the world. To try to understand the collective experience and plight of the Chinese by imagining the same things being done to the United States or Britain would horrify us out of our wits.

The general understanding among the imperialist nations that China must remain territorially intact, so that all of China could be open to exploitation by all of them – the understanding formulated in the notes on the Open Door – was not being observed. In July 1910 the Russians and the Japanese, who were more eager than their rivals for territorial expansion at China's expense, signed an agreement which implied that they would collaborate in their moves against China. Immediately afterwards Japan proceeded to complete her annexation of Korea, an independent nation friendly to China, whose territory she had occupied and controlled ever since the Sino–Japanese war of 1894–5. It was clearly a preliminary to an advance into the adjacent areas of China. The Russians followed this up with moves in the Mongolian region of China. Adopting the tone they had always done, they issued a series of rude notes and ultimatums to the Chinese, demanding from Peking the terms they wanted. There had been no dispute, and no discussion. The Chinese government on 27 March 1911 obligingly surrendered to the Russians. The British government then announced that 'Russia and Japan had special interests in Mongolia and Manchuria' and spoke of 'Japan's rights and special interests' in China. A British writer of the time quotes disapprovingly current Russian statements (1912) to the effect that 'Our time honoured policy . . . was founded on the axiom that Russia needs territorial expansion at the expense of her neighbours.' But Britain herself was playing the same game in order to get hold of parts of

China she wanted, in this case Tibet. She was not, however, very successful.

The kind of world order into which China had forcibly been incorporated was indeed a ruthless and cynical one. President Taft of the United States engaged in his 'dollar diplomacy' in language rather less crude that that of the Russians and the Japanese, but it was clear that the Americans, like the others, wanted to benefit themselves at China's expense. The Americans would rather see Japan commit aggression against China by seizing her north-eastern provinces than have the dynamic Japanese turning eastwards towards Central and South America. The British, who possessed territory in every continent, did not consider Japanese or Russian expansionism immoral or politically reactionary; they only wanted to see Russia expand away from areas in which the British Empire was naturally destined or ordained to grow. The Chinese could not find any of the guardians of the international order who would help to prevent China's being treated as a vast pool of disposable land, natural resources, labour and money. They could find no allies outside the leadership of the anti-imperialist movements. Sun had done all he could to establish solidarity with these movements, and help them when he could. But they could not as yet help China. Within the imperialist countries there were anti-imperialist liberals, socialists and humanitarians. But there were, then as now, very few people who were liberal in domestic matters who did not subscribe to the aggressive nationalism of their ruling classes. There was in those days no internationally organized 'anti-communist' crusade which could serve as a front for imperialist expansion and aggression. The rhetoric was different, but all the major powers were imperialist, and Sun's Three Principles threatened the security of the international order, as we could say today. There was no international organization through which the Chinese revolutionaries could link their struggle with the

83

struggle of others. The Chinese had to cope with the vast power of the countries which did not want to see any diminution of the status and rights of foreign officials, armies, missionaries, banks, industries, police and magistrates in China.

After the establishment of the republican government in Nanking on 1 January 1912, foreign governments had the opportunity of entering into relations with it. After the formal abdication of the Manchu ruling house they had another opportunity. The republicans had committed themselves to the creation of a modern, democratic China on lines similar to those on which western countries had developed. Yet Sun and his colleagues were under attack by the propaganda organs of the West. The verbal attack on Sun by J. O. P. Bland we have already quoted from earlier; another quotation will indicate the kind of arguments used:

No doubt but that, when the new flags flew and the guns were fired to celebrate the passing of the Manchus and the dawn of a new era, there were many, even amongst the level-headed merchant class, and certainly amongst the peasantry, who expected great and good things from the proclaiming of the Republic. Was not America a Republic, and therefore prosperous? Therefore, in Shanghai, Canton, Changsha and many another city, where the word 'Republic' meant to the people at large no more than the blessed word 'Mesopotamia', men embraced each other publicly and wept for joy at the coming of Liberty, Equality and Fraternity. As it was in Turkey in July 1908, so it was in China in February 1912 – men, weary of bad government, were fain to believe in this miracle, which was to abolish tyranny and corruption for ever; and so it came to pass that the queueless, frock-coated students of China were regarded as heralds and harbingers of the millennium, and welcomed with something approaching their own fervent enthusiasm. And they, on their side, made haste to proclaim ideals of republicanism, highly attractive to people whose knowledge of political economy is rudimentary. The merchant was to be delivered from lekin and the farmer from land tax; there would be less work and more pay for everyone; equal justice would be administered to all; a strong and united Republic would compel the respect of foreign nations, and exact reparations for encroachments upon Chinese territory. Small wonder that the terrified mandarins, gathering their impressions of the revolution from Young China's perfervid journalism, made haste to transfer their allegiance, so that city after city, and province after province, declared themselves republican almost without knowing it. . . .

The writer attacks the 'solemn academic debates of the Nanking Assembly ending in the adoption of national conscription, woman suffrage and other impossibilities . . .', and the fact that

women, wives and sisters of the emancipated, organize social and political movements of their own, demand the vote and enrol themselves, greatly daring, as volunteers in the army of the Republic. Ardently they seek for ways to relieve China of the pressure, if not the presence, of the European – to abolish his extra-territorial privileges, to restrict his rights of residence in the interior, to obtain jurisdiction over the Treaty Port Settlements and full fiscal autonomy; but Young China's Chauvinism has yet to acquire the discretion which Young Turkey had learned in the hard school of international experience. . . . Young China, as at present constituted, will pass, the shadowy fabric of a restless dream. An inevitable reaction will restore the ancient ways, the vital Confucian morality and that enduring social structure whose apex is the Dragon Throne. . . .[1]

All this is worth quoting at length because it undoubtedly reflects what the European (and American) communities in China were thinking and talking about in those days. The deeper, long-term aspirations and needs of the Chinese people, which Sun's programme expressed, issued in political practices and demands which were too radical even by the standards of the most 'advanced' democracies. Reactions like these also remind us of the interesting fact that western liberalism is horrified when it is confronted with the militant assertion of belief in the best of bourgeois ideals. A great and in many ways original Chinese leader had brought the greatest of the non-European nations to admire and seek to realize the model of a social and political order in which men and women were equal, free and united in common tasks. It was a momentous achievement, with great possibilities for the future of mankind, as any genuine democrat would have recognized. But Sun was to learn that he could not find influential allies among the liberals in the West. It was only after Yuan had demonstrated his contempt for the republican constitution, had Sung Chiao-jen assassinated and broken with the Kuomintang and with Sun that the western powers 'recognized' the new government. The US State Department declared the American government's support for the reorganization loan, which Yuan clearly had no authority (except that of his armed forces) to contract for, and in 1913 officially entered into diplomatic relations with it.

It is significant that there was one important European leader who responded very differently to the 1911 Revolution. He was a citizen of the most expansionist of China's imperialist enemies, but he was himself a revolutionary then in exile. It was Lenin. Lenin wrote in 1912 a long comment on an article by President Sun which was published in a Belgian socialist newspaper. It is a remarkable and generous tribute to Sun's greatness. Since some readers may not have easy access to Lenin's piece it is, again, worth our while to quote some of his remarks:

... Every line of Sun Yat-sen's platform breathes a spirit of militant and sincere democracy. It reveals a thorough understanding of the inadequacy of a 'racial' revolution. There is not a trace in it of indifference to political issues, or even of underestimation of political liberty, or of the idea that Chinese 'social reform', Chinese constitutional reforms, etc., could be compatible with autocracy. It stands for complete democracy and the demand for a republic. It squarely poses the question of the condition of the masses, of the mass struggle. It expresses warm sympathy for the toiling and exploited people, faith in their strength and in the justice of their cause.

Before us is the truly great ideology of a truly great people capable not only of lamenting its age-long slavery and dreaming of liberty and equality, but of *fighting* the age-long oppressors of China. . . .

86

Lenin goes on to analyse, in Marxist terms, the situation in China. Needless to say, it is a perceptive and prophetic analysis.[2] He is much more clear-cut and systematic in his account of what was happening in China than Sun Yat-sen was capable of being. But he is sharp enough to perceive in the Chinese Revolution of 1911 the 'heroism of the revolutionary masses'. We do not know if Sun got to hear about Lenin's comments on his work before the Bolshevik Revolution brought Lenin and his party to power in Russia.

Sun was in exile after the failure of 1913, and he was trying to find Japanese allies. His efforts did not lead to much. What Japanese groups were prepared to do would hardly have served the cause of the Chinese Revolution. Some of the proposals and plans for Japanese–Chinese collaboration in the economic development of China with which Sun's name was associated were poorly conceived. In so far as they had Sun's approval or serious interest, they are an indication that Sun's political wisdom was sometimes unreliable during the years he was in exile. His long-term views were sound. China was urgently in need of industrial development of the kind achieved under capitalist auspices in Europe and Japan. But the political relationship being what it was between China and every one of the major imperialist countries, Japanese-assisted development would not have built up the Chinese economy; it would have been the colonial form of development. Japanese economic penetration, great enough in the Treaty Ports and in the north-east, would have been even more deadly. After 1911 China's way forward could not have been by way of the old type of colonialism. We can see now, with the advantage of hindsight, that even in 1914 China was bound up with a more 'advanced' form of imperialist domination than that under which India was suffering. Internally, the masses working in China's pre-industrial economy were politically much more advanced and active than the rural masses were at a comparable stage of economic development in Europe. Japanese society was politically more backward than Chinese society.

What does all this mean? One cannot apologize for these discussions of politics. For we cannot tell the story of a great revolutionary without talking about the revolution – in this case the revolutions – he led. In the years following the 1913 debacle, the situation within China and the international situation called for political leadership in China which would not concentrate on restoring the 1912 Republic. The democratic revolution could be achieved only if there were Chinese who could take up the task of making a much more thorough-going revolution – a much profounder transformation than had been attempted in 1912. The way to deal with the danger from the imperialist powers was not to make compromises (as in 1911–12) but to unite and liberate China through revolutionary mass action. And this is what the Chinese people began to do in 1915.

The occasion arose when, on 18 January 1915, the Japanese government, following the well-established precedent of foreign powers in China, peremptorily presented the Yuan regime with a list of twenty-one demands. It had been done secretly, and Yuan appears to have yielded. The Twenty-One Demands, as they came to be called, went far beyond anything which any foreign government had yet tried to bully China into doing. They would have reduced China to the status of a Japanese protectorate. The news of the Japanese action leaked out and aroused such anger in China that the Japanese found themselves dealing with tougher opponents than the corrupt rulers in Peking. What had happened was that Yuan, confronted by the Japanese ultimatum and the fact that Japanese troops had been sent to China, surrendered on 9 May and concluded a treaty with the Japanese on 25 May. But in March a 'National Association of Comrades against

Japan' had been formed by the public and, in spite of Yuan's attempts to stop it, there was a boycott of Japanese-made goods which lasted until December. The fierce opposition to 'peaceful' foreign aggression which developed at this time was to become more widespread in the years to come, and cause the Japanese more trouble.

NOTES

1. J. O. P. Bland, op. cit., pp. 97 ff.
2. Reprinted in *The Land Question and the Fight for Freedom*, Moscow.

9   A New Revolutionary Commitment

During his exile in Japan between 1913 and 1916 Sun had the opportunity to make fresh plans in the light of what he and his colleagues had learnt from the mistakes of the past. It was the rather loose and ultra-democratic organization of the Tung-Meng Hui which had allowed different leaders to adopt widely differing and contradictory policies in the name of the same revolution, and even to abandon the very basis of the party platform – the Three Principles of the People. It was the loose thinking that went with that kind of organization which had led them to believe that a man like Yuan Shih-kai could be persuaded to respect parliament and the republican constitution. A different type of party was needed. In 1914 Sun reorganized the Kuomintang on new lines, so that it could work underground. He called it the Chinese Revolutionary Party. (Its Chinese name, Chung-hua Ko-ming-tang, has sometimes caused confusion.)

Those who sought membership in it had to be willing to accept the right of the Party head to make decisions for the Party, and to obey them. The basis principles on which the revolution would be fought were to be 'the people's rights' and 'the people's livelihood'. After the first stage of revolutionary war was successfully completed, the revolution would enter the second stage: this was seen as a transitional period of 'tutelage', during which the party members alone would exercise dictatorial power. Their task would be to transform society and thus create the conditions for a democratic, constitutional form of government, which was to be the completion of the revolution.

This summary makes Sun's efforts sound more amateurish than they in fact were. There were deficiencies in this kind of revolutionary organization, though it was not to these that some of the less politically-minded members of the former Kuomintang took objection. *They* did not like it that only members of the Ko-ming-tang, who had all to swear allegiance to the party, could have the power in the transitional period. They thereby showed their former lack of understanding of what a revolution is. Sun was grappling seriously with basic problems which all Third World countries have had to face since his time. His political dilemmas were a faithful and more often than not an intelligent reflection of the actual situation in China. When we consider what this situation was during those years, as well as the experience he had been through already, we can see how right he was, in his renewed career as a revolutionary, to concentrate on the problems of political organization for achieving radical change. He was also right not to theorize abstractly (he was not a systematic thinker) but to put his ideology and strategy into practical form. What the creation of the new Revolutionary Party lacked, however, was direct contact with the people of China.

Sun and his colleagues made several clandestine visits to China. But it was some time before he could go back without falling foul of Yuan and the other warlords, and their backers. While in Japan he wasted a great deal of time trying to change the whole course of Japanese history and politics by his exhortations and ingenuous manoeuvres. Of course, when he did return to China to work openly, the political alignments there were of the kind which did not make it possible for his party to start work. He sometimes tended to get entangled in the 'politics' of the order he knew he had to work to overthrow. Before we look at what he did, we should perhaps notice an important change in

91

Sun's life. It was his marriage to Soong Ching-ling – a marriage which was not merely of private significance but of historic and political significance. For Ching-ling was a new comrade, and she was to be one of the revolutionary heirs of Sun, and the conscience of the revolution. She may also have helped Sun to pay more attention than he had to what the younger generation of Chinese were doing.

Sun had been obliged as a youth to marry a girl selected by his parents. His first wife had no interest in his work and, though they had children, they did not make a home together. Both had been victims of the rotten social system which Sun had committed himself to overthrowing, but at the age of seventeen a Chinese peasant in the 1880s, even a rebel like Sun, could not have thought of defying established marriage customs. How unhappy Sun and his first wife were must be a matter of surmise. Sun was candid about his political life, but he did not wear his heart on his sleeve. As far as we know, when he and his first wife took a divorce they did it in the customary manner and with due care and dignity. He had known Ching-ling and her sisters from the time they were little children, for their father, Charles Soong, was a friend and a political supporter. Ching-ling, the second daughter, had been to high school and university in the United States. On her return she had told Sun that she wanted to join him and work for him. She had hero-worshipped him, and did not think of marriage. Sun appears to have fallen in love with her, and did not want their companionship to be the cause of gossip. He also did not want any scandal which could be used by enemies of the revolutionary movement, and had proposed marriage, as he had already divorced his first wife. They were married in October 1915. The young Madame Sun not only did some of the confidential secretarial work for her husband, but eventually became a distinguished political leader in her own right. Her parents were very angry at the marriage, and Sun lost their friendship. Some of those who attacked and slandered Sun because of his revolutionary politics appear to have found in the marriage (and the divorce before it) fresh opportunity for their criticisms. But no serious harm appears to have been done to the Suns. Whether or not they did an 'unchristian' thing we must consider later when we look at Sun's life as a whole.

In thinking mainly about the leaders of the Chinese Republic there is a danger of our getting too far away from the fundamental reality of China. If we succumbed to it we would have lost the context in which we have to place Sun's life. China was the four to five hundred million Chinese who suffered or hoped as they toiled in the fields, the streets, the rivers and the factories. It was mainly the hundreds of millions near the bottom of the hierarchy of oppression, who laboured on plots of land too small and too much exploited to provide them with the means of decent survival, or to enable them to pay their debts, their rent and their taxes. The gross poverty, the technological backwardness, the misery and discontent, and the need for radical change, had been great enough when Sun and his friend travelled through China in 1892, learning what life was like for the Emperor's subjects in provinces other than Kwangtung. They were even greater in the warlord period ushered in by Yuan Shih-kai's counter-revolution.

The rising middle class and foreign interests had been the social base on which Yuan and the warlords built their power. For the group of men who had made themselves the sole beneficiaries of the 1911 Revolution China was making progress in the right direction. The rising class consisted of those who had large land-holdings (and who served the foreign bankers, importers, exporters and industrialists), and the few Chinese owners of large businesses in the towns; it included those who controlled armies for whose services others would pay. It was good for them that in a few years there had been steep increases in the price of land, in rents, in the price of food and other commodities. During the anti-Japanese boycotts and demonstrations which followed Japan's Twenty-One Demands, Yuan had wanted the action against the Japanese called off. Some manufacturers found it both politic and profitable to turn the campaign into one for supporting native industries. They had a stake in the growing nationalist feeling. The anti-strike laws which Yuan passed benefited the Chinese capitalists as well as the foreign enterprises in China.

For the poor, however, these developments were not good. Rising prices and increased rents accelerated the process of pauperization in China. Hungry peasants unable to redeem their debts to the local moneylenders or pay the rent had to sell what little land they had. Half the 'farmers' who made up over ninety per cent of the population were landless. In the cities the coolies' standard of living fell, even though it had been incredibly low already. The opportunities for emigration were not as varied as they had once been. The World War was a special opportunity. The Allied Powers who were fighting in France were able to recruit coolies for menial labour there. They were first sent in 1916 to work in labour battalions, and by the end of the war about 200,000 of them were working in Europe, Iraq, Egypt and elsewhere for the French, British and American governments. In the countryside the changes of government in Peking and Nanking had done nothing to reduce the power of local despots; it was the same people as before who collected the taxes and had judicial and administrative power. In addition, the levies made by the warlords, and the growing anarchy in the country, made life increasingly insecure.

In 1912 Sun had written:

At present I am more interested in the social regeneration of my country than I am in questions of party and politics. Having finished the task of bringing about a political revolution, I am devoting my thought and energies to the reconstruction of the country in its social, industrial and commercial conditions. I have seen enough of the discord between capital and labour in western countries, and the misery that besets the multitudes of the poor, that I am desirous of forestalling such conditions in China. With industrial development there comes an increase of manufacturing, and with the change of conditions there is a danger of widely separating the working classes and those who possess the capital. I wish to see masses of the people improved in their conditions rather than to help a few to add power to themselves until they become financial autocrats.[1]

He had already relinquished the position of Provisional President when he wrote this for a foreign audience. Sun had seen to it that the constitution, which recognized the right of association, was passed before he resigned. But he was not there in power to ensure the workers could in fact enjoy the right, essential for their protection in a semi-feudal and capitalist society.

To eliminate poverty, to provide more work for people, to improve the technological and scientific standards in the country and to make it possible for China to withstand the pressures and attacks of the imperialist powers, China needed more industries, a modern transport system and people with new skills. Chinese who were enterprising enough to start and develop industries and to compete successfully with the foreign-owned industries and commercial enterprises were rendering a national service – as long as they did not join those who were exploiting and impoverishing the country. Sun did not see the rising capitalist class as the enemy. What he was against was the emergence of a ruling class like that to be found in the capitalist countries. But how was China to avoid the evils and inhumanity of the capitalist system? What was the new Chinese road to construction to be? Sun worked hard at these questions. He did extensive research on the subject, talked to people, wrote about it, proposed schemes. A truly revolutionary and original understanding of many of the issues taken up in our own day in studies of development, international aid, the military in developing countries, and so on, were crucial to the success of Sun's work during those years. In 1923 and 1924 his doctrines were to be given more systematic expression.

In 1917 Sun and a number of his colleagues came to the conclusion that the various cliques of civilian and military leaders who had set themselves up in power in various parts of China had to be brought to order by a central government which respected the constitution of the Republic. Worst of all was the situation in Peking. Yuan had died in 1916, and the generals who had been his henchmen carried on unchecked. The foreign powers found it very convenient to 'recognize' as *the* government of China a warlord-controlled regime which had no constitutional authority. This regime could therefore be forced to agree to policies and decisions binding on China as a whole. China's participation in the European war had been opposed in the country; it was a meaningless gesture. The Germans had been as nasty as the others, but the British, Russians, French and Japanese had harmed China much more than the Germans and the Austrians, and still threatened her. China's involvement in a distant war would, as Sun Yat-sen warned, only further the disintegration of the country. Nevertheless, the Peking regime declared war on Germany. But the military factions who were holding the country to ransom were marching their troops up and down within the country, rather than fighting a foreign enemy.

Those who wanted to restore constitutional rule by civilians decided therefore to break with the Peking regime and to set up a government in Canton. Members of parliament assembled in Canton and elected Sun Yat-sen as head of the new government. The Chinese Navy supported the new government, which was set up in August 1917. Subsequently, there were some changes in the form of government; Sun resigned his post and served as one of a committee of directors of the Canton government. All this must have been very confusing, especially as the

Canton government was under pressure from the various military factions in south and south-west China. For the mass of the Chinese people these moves and counter-moves, and the attempt to restore the constitution of the 1912 Republic, could not have seemed very important. Sun was deeply disappointed; the political bankruptcy of the men he had had to deal with and among whom he had to seek allies was evident. He was baffled. Writing books and giving lectures was important, but was it going to build up a vast country which had no government? He went to Shanghai in 1918. Writing about the first revolution he recalled that the salvation of the Chinese people and of the country had been the aim of those who worked and fought for it. But 'the result has been the opposite, and the Chinese people is becoming more and more oppressed, the country more and more unhappy.' He saw China going down a 'blind alley', and expressed his resolve to stir 'millions' of his fellow-countrymen to fight for China's reconstruction, and to 'create a government by the people, of the people and for the people. I believe in this, since I believe in the Chinese people.'

Sun, as we noted before, was a simple and unaffected person and spoke his mind freely. His surprising vagueness was due partly to his incorrigible faith in the capacity of people to be moved by great ideals, by patriotism and by appeals for social justice. But he was beginning, just about this time, to realize that his gentleness was mistaken. Much more important, he came to accept the fact that the contradictions in Chinese society could be resolved only by a much more radical revolution than he had yet been prepared to work for. He saw the futility of trying to subdue the forces of reaction by punitive military expeditions which led to domination by a new warlord clique. The militarists, bureaucrats and politicians were part of the structure which had to be destroyed before revolutionary construction could begin. The Kuomintang had to be reorganized. 'Henceforth our party should regard the mind and strength of the people as that of our party and it should use the mind and strength of the people in its struggles,' as he put it a few years later, when he spoke to old colleagues. He argued that failures of the past few years had been due not to lack of military strength but to lack of 'support of the people'; ideological and political work was necessary for building up a revolutionary party.

Important events in China and abroad had helped to confirm Sun's belief that the Three Principles could be realized only by a new kind of revolution. One of these events was the Bolshevik Revolution, and the tremendous changes it had effected in Russia; the kind of party he had conceived as necessary had proved to be successful there. Sun was in his fifties, but he was capable of developing his ideas and of sharing leadership with young revolutionaries who only partly looked to him for guidance. Perhaps it would be more correct to say that Sun developed into the leader of a second major revolution in China because he was humble enough to learn from students, workers and peasants.

Some of the new associates – men and women whom Sun sought out or who sought him out as they planned for revolutionary action – had led a series of movements from 1916 onwards. Cut off from Peking, and absorbed in provincial politics for some years, Sun had not until 1919 been involved in the remarkable intellectual and cultural revolution led by the students and teachers of China's great university in Peking. Sun's former Minister of Education, Tsai Yuan-pei, was its Vice-Chancellor. And Tsai had promoted in his university intellectual freedom and creativity such as China had not witnessed for a long time. It is difficult for us in Western Europe and North America, who have not experienced anything more than a severely circumscribed liberal democracy, to imagine what an impact the democratic convictions of the Chinese revolutionaries had on Chinese institutions and Chinese society. Tsai did not want students to enter the university in order to get good appointments or become rich, but to pursue true learning. In his administrative policy he had as one of his principles that the university was an institution for academic research, aimed at the creation of a new civilization. He also insisted on 'true academic freedom'. One historian describes thus the way in which his liberal and progressive policies were implemented:

> . . . Professors with divergent points of view were brought into the institution. Various study and advisory groups among the faculty were established. The university was in the main governed by professors rather than administrators or officials. Students were permitted to take part in political activities as individuals. . . . Students' self-government was encouraged by Tsai and student societies for study, speech, discussion, publication, recreation, social service, athletics, and other activities, including a students' bank, a consumers' cooperative organization, and a museum, were established. A work-and-study programme similar to that which had been tried in France was also founded in the university. A spirit of equality was introduced into the institution. The previous barriers between students and professors as well as between them and janitors or workers were to a certain extent removed. The moral standards of the students were greatly improved . . . Of all Tsai's innovations at Peking University, perhaps the most significant was his practice of permitting the coexistence of divergent opinions. . . .[2]

Even now, half a century later, it is impossible to read about the vigorous and creative intellectual life of Peking University without feeling some of the excitement its members must have felt. The faculty was a galaxy of great talents – the best-known names in the West today being Li Ta-chao, Chen Tu-Hsiu, Hu Shih and Lu Hsun. Conservatives as well as radicals had equal freedom. But it had not been many years before that Peking had been the centre of the most conservative learning and morality. Now journals, books, lectures and debates in Peking University stirred intellectuals and others all over China to new ways of thought, new conceptions of society, new attitudes towards traditional ways and authority. The conservative views were the familiar ones and, however well defended, failed to carry conviction among those who did not regard China as a museum. The stilted writing admired by the traditionalists was attacked, and new literary movements, bringing poetry and essay-writing close to the idiom and vocabulary of common speech, flourished; philosophical and ethical traditions were exposed to searching and irreverent scrutiny and found wanting; there was a new emphasis on youth, on change, on creativity, on exploration, on experiment.

There were attempts to suppress this freedom. The conservatives who felt threatened naturally claimed that morality and order were being put in danger, and tried to use the power of the government to stop what was going on. If they had known what the historic consequences of Tsai's university policies would be they would have tried harder. A whole generation of talented students was influenced by the teachers of that time. Chen Tu-Hsiu edited, and he and Li Ta-chao contributed to, a journal called *New Youth*. When Li Ta-chao heard the news about the Bolshevik Revolution in Russia he was profoundly moved. Li was only the first of that brilliant group who found in Marxist revolution the answer to China's economic and social problems. The intelligent and intense curiosity about the world outside the view of Chinese traditional thought – the *whole* world – developed by the new type of university represented the true opening of China. It was the opening of the Chinese mind to what was most valuable and instructive in contemporary life. We may remember how Sun had to spend more than a year around 1897 doing research and having discussions with people in Europe; he had then learnt to be critical of western society, while still seeking to create a democratic China. The intellectual revolution during the years of the First World War and just afterwards made the Chinese much more aware politically than they had ever been in modern times.

Since the end of the war some of the coolies who had been recruited by the French, British and Americans had been repatriated. Among these had been several young intellectuals who wanted to study abroad but had been too poor to afford to pay for themselves. They had lived and worked among the labourers, and sometimes been labourers themselves. They had learned the art of teaching illiterates, and the coolies had thus made close contact with politically conscious Chinese radicals. The barrier between the scholars and writers on the one hand, and the labourers on the other, had been breached. The revolution in literature and political thinking enabled scholars and writers to engage in political discussion. The May Fourth Movement showed how important these new developments could be. When the Versailles Peace Conference announced its decisions on questions affecting Chinese territory which the Germans had, previous to 1914, seized, it was discovered that the British, French and American governments were handing over to Japan areas in Shantung the Germans had seized. Though China had been an ally of these countries, the decision was made because of a secret deal between the French, British and Japanese governments. On the logic and the morality of such a decision it is easy to make up one's mind. But the fact was that the protests of the Chinese delegates in Paris had little effect on the decisions made by Wilson, Lloyd George and Clemenceau. The regime in Peking, though it had no constitutional validity, was controlled by pro-Japanese elements, and it purported to act for the Chinese Republic in making a secret deal with the Japanese.

The response of the Chinese students and workers to all this far exceeded that of 1915, and in fact marked a turning point in Chinese history. On 4 May 1919 there was a big demonstration in Peking, in the careful organization of which Peking University students played the leading part. What the students did for their country won them the respect and gratitude of their elders in Peking and all over the country. Students in other cities – Tientsin, Shanghai, Changsha, Wuhan and many other places – organized their own demonstrations and political action. There were boycotts of Japanese goods. Workers went on strike, demonstrating not only their patriotism but also a new capacity for organization. Women emerged again as active participants in national politics, and resumed the movement for emancipation and equality. It is no exaggeration to say that the country came to life politically all of a sudden. The effects of the May Fourth Movement were immense.

The New Culture Movement and the May Fourth Movement, and the transformations which followed, occurring at about the time when the Bolshevik Revolution had shown what the people in an imperialist country could do to transform its politics and ideology, provided Sun with opportunities he could not have imagined in 1915. He drew new life and ideas from the cultural and political renaissance. There was also a new appreciation of Sun's work; and in the early 1920s people were much more ready to believe in the importance and possibility of transforming the people's livelihood (the third of Sun's Three Principles) than they had been ten years earlier. They sought Sun out in Shanghai, and had long talks with him. New leaders were emerging – men of different calibre to that of Huang Hsing and Sung Chiao-jen. What the old revolutionaries had rejected, the younger revolutionaries and masses eagerly welcomed. Li Ta-chao and Chen Tu-hsiu, younger men like Mao Tse-tung and Chou En-lai, were beginning to plan for a Chinese Revolution in terms rather different from those in which Sun had been thinking. Sun did not feel threatened by these developments. He grew in political understanding, and his own political theories began to undergo a process of modification and grew richer in significance.

Sun's own words are not easy to paraphrase, and it would be useful to quote a letter he wrote on 29 January 1920 to some overseas members of the Kuomintang:

Since the students of the Peking University launched the May Fourth Movement, the youthful patriots in China have been adopting new ideas for the modernization of all enterprises. Consequently, with the support of public opinion in every walk of life, there has been a rapid growth of free expressions of views and thoughts. The new publications which have been sponsored by the enthusiastic young people have one after another made their appearance to meet the needs of the changing times. Each one of such publications has, within its sphere, made a full contribution as well as a deep impression on the society.

The renaissance movement which is taking place in China today is indeed a gigantic ideological revolution unprecedented in our history. Actually it owed its inception to the initiative of a handful of thinking writers. Gradually we see that throughout the length and breadth of the country the brilliance of their pens has been radiating; the intellectual waves have been surging; and the conscience of the people has been awakened to such a degree that a number of patriotic activities were undertaken even at the risk of one's own life.

If our efforts along these lines could continue to develop, the achievements are bound to be imposing, enduring and far-reaching. The success of the revolution which our party (Kuomintang) desires to see accomplished will have to depend upon the revolutionization of our ways of thinking. That is why military strategy stresses the tactics of *striking-at-the* heart while *transforming-the-heart* is likewise a popular watchword. Indeed, it is this Chinese renaissance movement to which I am attaching the highest value.[3]

This report tells us why Sun's prestige and influence continued to grow among the young. His own political evolution was taking him towards a new alliance. The mounting anger against the imperialist powers was something he had himself been experiencing. It had been part of Sun's idealism and belief in the possibilities for good in others that he had had for a long time tried to get foreign sympathy for China by appeals to the conscience and good sense of the West. He had for a long time seen how seriously the practices and policies of the imperialist powers were ruining China. If he could have got the governments and public opinion of these countries to see and feel about these policies and practices as the Chinese did, then China

103

would be relieved of part of the oppression from which she suffered. What it took time for Sun to see was that as long as he appealed to the consciences of people and to principles he was not taken seriously. It was very much in the interests of the foreign powers to assist the warlord regimes with money, arms and diplomatic support. It would not have made sense for the British, Japanese, French and other foreign powers who exercised power and authority within China to follow the example of the now anti-imperialist government in Russia, which in 1919 issued a friendly 'Manifesto to the Chinese People' (known also as the Karakhan Declaration) and followed it up with action. The restoration of all the territory seized from China by the Tsarist governments was announced and extraterritorial 'rights' were renounced.

The propaganda effect of the Soviet Russian move alone was tremendous. There was gratitude. There was hope of change. There was great interest in the politics of the Russian Revolution. The western powers and Japan could, if they had wanted, have countered the Soviet move by a change of policy on *their* part. They could have unilaterally withdrawn their armed forces from China, closed down foreign postal services and radio stations in China, restored tariff autonomy to China, relinquished their 'extra-territorial' privileges, surrendered the concessions, leased territories and zones of foreign administration forcibly acquired in the past, promised not to enter into secret deals on matters vitally affecting China or Far Eastern questions, promised also to respect China's right to be a major party in making decisions affecting East Asia, and agreed to stop interfering in China's internal politics. They did not lack opportunity to win Chinese support and friendship. If they did not want to do it unilaterally, they could have done these things at the Washington Conference, which began at the end of 1921.

At the Washington Conference the powers China had to contend with were the United States, Britain, France and

104

Japan. Dealing with them was a China which, as *The Times* had suggested before the Conference, 'from the point of view of international relations [*sic*], is, in her present divided state, largely a fiction'. The Conference gave the Chinese the only answer that could have been expected. The Chinese delegation was oppressed and bullied, and sometimes treated with contempt. The delegation was, of course, the only one the imperialist powers would 'recognize'. Its right to demand changes in China's international status could conveniently be questioned, when the demands became insistent. For it was the foreigners, it could be and was claimed, and not the weak and corrupt Peking regime, which watched over the true interests of the 'the Chinese people'. In regard to the Chinese demands, *The Times*, true to form, wrote about 'the doubts and questionings among persons acquainted with Far Eastern affairs'.

The French delegate gave expression to some of these doubts by bluntly asking Mr Koo and his colleagues on what authority they affect to speak for China as a whole, at a time when it is notorious that the feeble government in Peking exercises no power and little influence over a great part of the eighteen provinces, not to say anything of the other parts of the Empire [*sic*]. The answer that the Government of Peking is the only recognized government in China does not meet the inquiry. The matter of real moment to the Conference is not what the Mandarins in Peking, or what the western educated reformers in the South, desire, but what the people of China – the dumb, industrious peaceful millions of China – desire. . . .[4]

This comment, candidly claimed as the view of 'those who know Asiatics', indicates what satisfaction the Chinese got. Sun had an unofficial representative at the Conference, but the American delegation objected to his attempts to influence the Peking delegation. There were, as there are today, many of 'those who know Asiatics' who would have believed that it would not be to the good of 'China' that a revolutionary like Sun, who had made up his mind that the unification of China was necessary to fight imperialism, should be encouraged. Sun was himself to have some serious confrontations with the power of the British in his own home territory. In 1922 the Canton government wanted the customs revenue from South China to be handed over to it. This proper and reasonable request was turned down by the British. The government then informed the British consul that it would take steps to collect the revenue. The British as a matter of policy paid only the Peking regime. In response to the Canton government's decision to assert its authority the British moved gunboats into position close to Canton. Sun was forced to submit to this gunboat diplomacy, as his predecessors had in the 1840s and 1850s. On another occasion Sun dared the British to carry out their threats. In 1924 the Canton government found itself threatened by a right-wing organization of merchants and gentry, headed by a man from Hong Kong, who was working for the Hong Kong and Shanghai Banking Corporation in Canton. The Canton government seized a cargo of arms meant for the paramilitary organization created by these opponents of Sun and his policies. On 29 August the British consul-general threatened Sun with 'immediate action' if the 'volunteers' were attacked, and again the gunboats flying the Union Jack entered Cantonese waters. Sun took up the challenge, making it clear in his angry notes to the local diplomats and to Prime Minister Ramsay MacDonald in London that he understood very well that in their support for counter-revolution in China the British had for years been aiming to overthrow him. The 'volunteers' were engaged in battle and beaten, and their attempt to close shops were frustrated. This was a defeat for Britain.

Sun's success on that occasion was due to the strength he had acquired politically because of increasing working-class support. The workers had formed a Labour Organizations' Army, to make up for the lack of military force at

Sun's disposal; the formation of this workers' armed force was authorized by Sun and his progressive Minister of Labour, Liao Chung-kai. The printing workers played their part by declaring a strike in support of their demand that the daily newspapers stop supporting the enemies of Sun. The active political role played by the workers was a new factor in the growth of Sun's strength during those years. Ever since the formation of the 1917 Canton government in support of the republican constitution, the trade union movement had grown in the south. There had been a wave of strikes in 1919 when there had been a warlord threat to Kwangtung. When Sun after election by parliament was inaugurated President of the Canton government in May 1921 the working class joined in the celebrations. Sun was leader of the Kuomintang again, and the character of the Kuomintang was changing as a result of the active support which politically militant workers in Canton were giving it. In January 1922, after negotiations with the British colonial authorities had broken down, the seamen's union called its Hong Kong members out on strike. The declaration of martial law, the proscribing of unions concerned in this and the sympathy strikes, and the attempt to use blacklegs all failed to break the strike. The strikers were in a strong position partly because of the solidarity shown by the unions in China and the help given by the workers in Canton. The Kuomintang government's loan to them, though not intended to be taken as intervention in the strike, was useful at a time when, with the spread of the strikes in Hong Kong (over 120,000 workers having stopped work), the Canton workers had to provide hospitality.

The Canton government's tolerance and even encouragement of radical working-class activity, and its permission for an All China Labour Congress to be held in Canton in April 1922, should not be taken to signify any commitment on Sun's part to encourage class war against the capitalists. The anti-imperialist aims of the militant workers were in accordance with new trends in the Kuomintang. And Sun's increasing interest in and awareness of the fact that Chinese coolies were willing to assume political responsibilities had not in 1922 issued in any clear-cut policy of support for working-class militants. But the rise of Liao Chung-kai, and Sun's confidence in him, was a development of great promise for the Kuomintang. Sun, and his old comrade Liao, had come a long way in the ten years since 1912. It had become clear that the Three Principles could be realized not by a restoration of what had been destroyed by Yuan and the warlords but by a new democratic revolution.

NOTES

1. Quoted in Martin, p. 156.
2. Chow Tse-tsung, *The May Fourth Movement*, Stanford University Press 1967, pp. 50–1.
3. Wunsz King, *China at the Paris Peace Conference in 1919*, St John's University Press, Jamaica, NY 1961, pp. 38–9.
4. Quoted by Wunsz King, *China at the Washington Conference, 1921–1922*, St John's University Press, Jamaica, NY 1963, pp. 38–9.

10 The New Democratic Revolution 1924—

It was in 1922 that Sun and his wife, Ching-ling, came close to being killed by the man who was supposed to be the Minister of War of the Canton government. Sun had been persuaded to take refuge on one of the ships of the Chinese navy, and his wife escaped because she had disguised herself effectively. Traditionally, soldiers were held to be the meanest form of human life, and the experience of Sun, and of the Chinese people, burdened with the support of about a million troops, justified the traditional view. The treachery of yet another military commander must have reminded Sun once more that in his revolutionary thinking and planning he had failed to cope adequately with the problem of a revolutionary army. Sun had never been foolish enough to think that the Chinese could be freed from what he called their 'triple oppression' by a non-violent revolution. He had, however, tried to win over to his cause, by political persuasion and patriotic appeals, the military forces at the disposal of those who were oppressing and ruining China. He was now dealing with warlords who were wily politicians, whose capacity for deceiving the people was greater than Sun's for undeceiving them about what the warlords were up to. The President's insistence that 'soldiers should be converted into labourers and their weapons . . . replaced with tools' helped to send him again into exile in Shanghai, in August 1922.

Radically new political plans were taking shape then in the minds of Sun and his close associates. But in the meantime the general, Chen, who had betrayed him in Canton, had to be dealt with. Sun was, as always, a resolute fighter as well as a peacemaker and statesman. So great was his prestige and his authority that he was able to organize the movement of several armies towards Chen's positions, driving him out of Canton by January 1923. Chief-of-staff of one of these armies was a talented officer called Chiang Kai-shek, whose continued loyalty to Sun had already marked him out as the man through whom the Canton military government, as it came to be in 1923, was to have its own officers' training academy and its own military command. Back in Canton, Sun again made it clear that military forces in China would have to be reduced before reconstruction could begin. In the south Sun assigned the army commanders (all independent warlords) different areas, and ordered that they should not move without his orders. We have cause to wonder at the power that Sun was able to wield. The warlords in the north, in spite of all the wealth and soldiers at their disposal and the foreign support they had, were beginning to realize that in this civilian revolutionary leader they had met their match. All the intrigues they tried failed to budge Sun. They knew that eventually Sun would unite the country, and leave no room for them to enjoy their power and their wealth. The detailed story of what happened in North China in 1922 and 1923 is as sordid as that of the actions and policies of the foreign powers in China. The details of the intimidation, the massive bribery and corruption and the personalities need not detain us, though they added up in the end to the total collapse of the attempts to pretend that the warlord cliques of the north represented the Chinese Republic, and thus made it more urgent than ever for Sun to take some action to get control over the whole of China.

Sun had made mistakes and had for two or three years shown that he was politically confused. Yet here he was, in his fifty-seventh year, with an inescapable responsibility. It

110

is difficult for us, without a great effort, to reach an understanding of the crisis in China, and the tremendous importance at that moment of the direction that would be given to China's development. Sun was called to take the leadership. It was the kind of mandate given by the social situation, by public opinion, and by the way in which offers of help and support were made to him at that time. The social situation is often thought of by us in the West as a static condition. It is in fact hardly ever anything but dynamic, calling for creative action. In China, in a society which was at different levels entering several periods of historical development, the reading of the social situation was much more difficult than it would have been in a society in which economic, cultural, political and scientific development had been more even. China's situation at that time, and even now, is unlike that in western European countries or the United States; it resembles that in other major Third World societies. It was remarkable that Sun had the independent understanding of China which enabled him to make what we now know was the correct decision.

In August 1922, when Sun was in Shanghai, he was planning not only his return to Canton, but the transformation of the Kuomintang into a party which could organize and lead the next phase of the Chinese Revolution. Li Ta-chao appears to have visited him there and told him that he wanted to join the Kuomintang, while still remaining a member of the Communist Party of China, of which he was one of the founders. This was agreed to. Sun himself had been thinking of reorganizing the new Kuomintang on the model of the Soviet Russian Communist Party. And he had to think of the implications of having members of the CPC, itself formed on the Bolshevik model, joining the Kuomintang. To have a man of Li's character and abilities in the revolutionary government in Canton was to have a great addition of strength and popular support. Li, one of the greatest men in modern China, became a close colleague of Sun;

111

other able and devoted members of the CPC followed him and joined the new Kuomintang, while still remaining active members of their own party. Sun's revolution benefited from the experience of these men and women.

What can we make of Sun's attitude to Marxian communism and to communists? He did not, of course, fear them, and he had no reason to. Fear of revolutionary overthrow by workers, peasants and revolutionary intellectuals can be seriously experienced only by those who live by exploiting and oppressing them, and by those who share the ideology of feudal despotism or capitalism. That is, it is natural to those who belong to the classes threatened or are loyal to them, such as the police, journalists, teachers, military and so on. Sun was already himself convinced that the imperialists, militarists and their agents were the cause of China's ills, and that their power had to be overthrown. He had some commitment to support Chinese who strove, in the face of these evils, to help to develop China industrially and culturally. But he had no loyalty to any class threatened by a revolution; he only disagreed with the CPC on specific issues. It is necessary for us to understand that he had not allowed himself to get westernized in his outlook, values and loyalties. It would be absurd to ask if he had the anxieties about 'the communists' produced in those who have been subjected for many decades to intensive propaganda and campaigns of misrepresentation; the vast majority of the people who live in the Third World can hardly be expected to have the same class interests and hatreds as British or American businessmen, and the products of the educational system and culture of capitalist-ruled societies. It was most natural that in 1918 Sun should write to Lenin, wishing success to the revolutionaries, in the face of attacks by the very forces which were and had been China's enemies too. It was natural for him to have a correspondence in 1921 with Chicherin, the Soviet Foreign Minister and to be very interested to hear from a European communist about the problems that the Bolshevik leaders were having in carrying out their revolutionary programme in view of the backwardness of the Russian economy. Sun was himself grappling with some of the questions which Lenin had to face. And it would have been surprising if he had not asked the Soviet envoy, Joffe, to call on him at a time when he believed that the Chinese revolutionaries needed to work more closely than before with the Russian revolutionaries. The communist bogey was a problem for those threatened by China's liberation, not for Sun. It must be noted that during that period Stalin's efforts to get control were only beginning to catch Lenin's attention; the purges, tortures, concentration camps and other features of the Tsarist-style despotism with which Stalinism destroyed the good name of the Bolsheviks was to come long after.

Some of the foreign communists who visited China or went there on political missions were not very impressive men. Most of them were hardly comparable in quality and achievement to the Chinese Marxists. They were, however, internationalists, and men who believed in the possibility of creating a new world order in which the oppression of peasants and workers and colonial peoples could be brought to an end. They were also men through whom, at the beginning, relations could be maintained between the Chinese and the Russian revolutionaries on the basis of equality and mutual respect. To understand China's development in its proper context we have to ignore the theories of Leninist conspiracy by which China was 'lost' to the West and Japan. Sun acted openly, and with authority and dignity. He knew that what happened in China was the business of the Chinese, and he made decisions as the responsible head of a Chinese revolutionary government. There is no evidence to support the propaganda of sinologists who have made it out that the decisions affecting China were made by Soviet agents. Indeed, the foreigners whom Sun consulted about the structure of the new Kuomintang and the revolutionary programme did little more than provide the advice and information asked for. Where Soviet envoys were on a mission, they made offers and requests on behalf of the Soviet government or, on occasion, negotiated on behalf of their government. Sun bears responsibility, as leader of the revolutionary Kuomintang, for policies and decisions of that period. After his discussions with Adolf Joffe they issued a communique which included this statement:

> Dr Sun is of the opinion that, because of the non-existence of conditions favourable to their successful application in China, it is not possible to carry out either Communism or even the Soviet system in China. M. Joffe agrees with this view; he is further of the opinion that China's most important and most pressing problems are the completion of national unification and the attainment of full national independence. With regard to these great tasks, M. Joffe has assured Dr Sun of the Russian people's warmest sympathy for China, and of (their) willingness to lend support.[1]

Sun knew better than the more idealistic faction in the CPC which dreamed of the 'industrial proletariat' leading a revolution and taking power in a pre-industrial society like China. The Three Great Policies basic to the formation of the new Canton government issued from deeply-held principles. Sun would not accept a coalition between the Kuomintang and the CPC, as though the Kuomintang was a representative of the capitalists. For him the Kuomintang was a revolutionary, left-wing party through which workers and peasants could fight for the realization of socialism. But the Three Principles of the People could be observed only by a government which was allied with the labouring masses, which worked with the members of the Communist Party of China and which had an alliance with the world's leading revolutionary force, the Soviet Union. Sun, Liao and their close associates were not sectarian in their outlook. When the Kuomintang was reorganized, Li Ta-chao

114

became a member of the presidium, and leading members of the CPC, including Mao Tse-tung, were elected to the central committee. Chiang Kai-shek, the leading military man in the Kuomintang, was sent in 1923 by Sun to learn from the Soviet Union how the Red Army was organized and other matters which would help him to set up a military academy. He came back and established the Whampoa Academy, and a young communist of great ability, Chou En-lai, was appointed by the government to be political director at Whampoa. Mao started working for the Canton revolutionary government among the peasantry. And Liao Chung-kai, who was the equivalent of Minister of Labour, was a Kuomintang leader who won great support from the industrial workers.

For many years Sun had worked on the assumption that with a firm base in Kwangtung it would be possible to complete the revolution throughout the country. So far this had been only partly confirmed in practice. An expedition to the north, to subdue the warlords and liberate the people under them, and to unify the country was again planned, and it was to prove successful. Its success was due not so much to the military strength of the Canton government but to the enthusiastic support of the masses. The sincerity of Sun's championship of the poor and oppressed in China was never in question. But, for the first time, the Canton revolutionary government gave clear organizational expression to this concern. A passage from the Declaration of the First National Congress of the reorganized Kuomintang (January 1924) defined a policy which must have had a strong appeal for workers and peasants:

As to the third of the Principles of the People, the principle of livelihood for the people comprises two major aims: equalization of landholdings and regulation of capital. To achieve economic equilibrium we must no longer permit to a minority among our people a monopoly in land ownership. The state must regulate the ownership, use, and purchase of land as well as tax levies on land.

115

Such regulations implement the principle of equality in property rights.

To prevent private capitalism from controlling the people's livelihood, the state will manage and control all banks, railroads and ship lines, and all other large-scale enterprises. With the regulation of landholdings and the regulation of capital we establish socialism on a secure foundation.

Our farmers will understand us when we assert that agriculture is the basic source of China's wealth; and, at the same time, of all classes in the nation, farmers have endured the greatest hardships. Under the Kuomintang the state will grant land to all landless and tenant farmers and also issue tools to work the land. Moreover, the state will repair irrigation works, instruct farmers in the rotation of crops, and assist farmers in the cultivation of new lands. By establishing and managing banks for farmers, the state will assist those who lack capital and have now been enslaved by enforced loans at exorbitant rates of interest. Ultimately farmers will enjoy the good life they deserve.

Chinese labourers without security and protection may be assured that it is the express policy of the Kuomintang to protect workers and to find employment for those who are out of work. Since poverty-stricken farmers and labourers exist everywhere in China and share in the common misery, they understand the need of liberation from oppression and should be able to understand the need to drive out the imperialists. Since the success of the nationalist revolution depends on cooperation from farmers and labourers, the Kuomintang must actively assist farmers' and workers' movements, and also subsidize such efforts. We must also work untiringly to persuade farmers and workers to become members of the Kuomintang, making clear to them that since the Kuomintang is fighting against the imperialists and the warlords and all privileged classes, the nationalist revolution is also a revolution to emancipate farmers and labourers. Farmers and labourers participating in the work of the Kuomintang will be working for their own best interests.[2]

We have here echoes of the definitions of the other Principles – those of nationalism and democracy. There was unmistakably a declaration of war on imperialist interests in China when the revolutionaries in Canton prepared for action. In 1925 and 1926 the people of China rose up in a revolution of a kind never before seen in China. There was the May Thirteenth Movement. The action of

116

peasants and workers all over south and central China ensured the success of the northern expedition, and the revolutionary capital was moved to Wuhan. In Hankow the British Concession was peacefully 'liberated' by the workers; the reversal of China's colonial history had begun. Early in 1927 the Kuomintang supporters in Shanghai took control of the city. The warlord armies in south and central China were defeated. Sun's vision of a unified China was fast becoming a reality.

If Sun had lived he might have been in Peking, establishing the kind of national government which could implement the programme of the Kuomintang. But the successes we have been describing were posthumous ones. Sun had left Canton with his wife at the end of 1924 to visit Shanghai and Peking, in the hope of bringing about unity without having to resort to war. Sun had hopes that a national conference might be held, at which workers, peasants, political parties, businessmen, students, educational institutions, armies (though not warlords) and other groups could be represented. Sun was a sick man, and the tremendous reception he received in Shanghai and Peking must have tired him. In any case, he had an operation for cancer, and in early March of the next year composed his political Will and Testament. In it he said that his forty years of political struggle for the Chinese Revolution had convinced him that 'to attain this goal, the people must be aroused' and that 'we must associate ourselves in a common struggle with all the peoples of the world who treat us as equals'. He added that 'the revolution is not yet finished', and spoke of the need to abolish the unequal treaties. He also, before he died, sent a letter to the leaders of the Soviet Union.

For China, though not for the interests threatened by his revolutionary activity, Sun's death just at that time was a disaster. The efforts of counter-revolutionary forces to take over the Kuomintang and reverse its policies became more intense after Sun's death. In August 1926 the popular Liao

Chung-kai was assassinated; and it came out that Kuomintang colleagues were implicated in the attempt to remove this man who had worked very closely with Sun. Finally, in April 1927, the Commander-in-Chief of the Kuomintang armies, General Chiang Kai-shek, staged a coup d'état just when the revolutionaries were greatly excited by their successes. Peasants and workers who had been largely responsible for the successes were massacred, literally in tens of thousands. Chiang was no ordinary militarist; he was intelligent, a good organizer and a brave soldier, and he was ruthless. The counter-revolution was well organized, and the undoing of the revolution systematic.

Had Sun been alive would Chiang have turned traitor? Even if Chiang had, could Sun have fought him successfully, and saved the revolution? We can say with certainty that Sun would have had no hesitation in organizing his forces for the destruction of Chiang's power. We can also be certain that Chiang and his supporters (who were Chinese as well as foreigners) would not have been able to transform the Kuomintang into a right-wing organization. Sun may have gone the way of Li Ta-chao, who was executed by the warlord who ruled in Peking. But Stalin's functionaries would never have been allowed to interfere, as they did in 1927, and make things difficult for the revolutionaries.

There are other questions which come to mind. Should we hold Sun responsible for his choice of Chiang as military commander? Chiang became very popular in the West and Japan after his coup, and the question does not appear to make sense. But, as Soong Ching-ling and others pointed out at the time, he stood for everything that Sun was fighting against. It does appear that it was only in the course of the two years between Sun's death and his counter revolution that Chiang's political loyalties changed. He went over to the gentry. He did not succeed in destroying the Chinese Revolution, however. Sun did not fail. It was the men he brought into his administration in Canton in 1924 who took up the leadership of the Chinese Revolution and defeated the counter-revolutionaries.

NOTES

1. Quoted in Huang Sung-kang, *Lu Hsun and the New Culture Movement of Modern China*, Amsterdam 1957, p. 100.
2. Li Chien-nung, op. cit., pp. 454–5.

11 A Humble Man

'Don't make trouble for the Christians,' Sun Yat-sen is reported to have said as he was dying.[1] These were strange words for a man whose life-long concern was for the poor and oppressed in his country. Among them there were very, very few Christians. Sun was not a person who thought and acted in a sectarian way, and he never, like most Christians, thought of himself as separate from or different from those who were not Christians. That those words of his were necessary must have made him very sad. And which Christian can honestly deny that that appeal for clemency is necessary in many other countries? In country after country in the Third World one has only to search among the counter-revolutionaries, the agents of imperialist or neocolonialist oppression, the defenders of privilege and reaction to find the Christians. This is a troublesome fact for Christians who are on the side of the poor and oppressed.

There are theological sophistries which will enable one to get over such difficulties, of course. But the fact is that among those fighting for the victims of oppressive political and economic systems Christians have rightly earned a reputation for unreliability and even treachery. If Sun had been a more conventional kind of Asian Christian one cannot imagine him playing the role that he played in the history of our age. Unless we acknowledge this we cannot honestly 'claim' him as one of the great Christians of the modern age. We cannot also, unless we admit the justice of the charge that Christians have recently been generally unreliable in revolutionary situations, appreciate the fact that all his life Sun never denied his Christian faith. This faith was something in which his whole life was rooted. At a critical moment in his life, when he was imprisoned in the Chinese Legation in London in 1896, and facing what looked like certain death, he did something which may not have made sense to many of the people among whom he spent most of his life.

In those days of suffering I only beat my heart and repented and earnestly prayed. For six or seven days I prayed incessantly day and night. The more I prayed the more earnest I was in my prayer. On the seventh day I felt suddenly comforted. I was absolutely without fear. The state of being comforted and feeling brave came to me unconsciously. This was the result of prayer. How fortunate I was to have received the Grace of God.[2]

This is a very rare glimpse into Sun's life. Sun could articulate his experience in terms intelligible to other Christians. No doubt, what he was touched by on that occasion and throughout his life is available to all men, and explains the remarkable courage and integrity of those who would find such epithets embarrassing. We are all naturally curious about what made a great man like Sun Yat-sen 'tick'. But his secret will perhaps remain inviolate. For his friendship with the Cantlie's all admirers of Sun must be grateful. James Cantlie's unaffected admiration for Sun tells us a great deal about his hold over men. The story of Sun's political career does not make sense unless this quality is taken into account. By all the ordinary standards of the political analyst and the historian Sun should not be in the history books. He was not a great political thinker. He was not a military strategist. He was not a subtle negotiator, or a man who knew how to make good use of the weaknesses of his adversaries. He did not inherit leadership. He seemed all the time to be trying and failing. The hostile biographers and detractors have thought that their job was easy. Yet Sun's monument is greater than that of any other person in the twentieth century, except for that of Mao

121

Tse-tung. Some of the values and qualities which make their country so distinguished, even unique, today the Chinese owe partly to Sun. Chairman Mao said in 1956:

> ... He left to us a great deal of political thought that has been beneficial to us.
> Apart from a handful of Chinese reactionaries all modern Chinese are successors to Mr Sun's revolution. ...

He also spoke of Sun as a 'humble man'. We can say that that humility has been infectious. Perhaps it is only a people like the Chinese who could have responded to Sun's call to seek a better road to independence, prosperity and greatness than any other nation has taken. Mao is the greater leader, undoubtedly, but Sun's influence on Mao was profound, for Sun spoke for what was best in the Chinese people. Perhaps we were inaccurate in calling Sun idealistic. He was thinking of a China which could not, in the material and social conditions of his own time, be immediately realized. But he was far-seeing in speaking to a China which is no longer weak and backward. In a country which still listens to what wise and good men say, Sun's pioneering work is gratefully acknowledged, and his ideals still appear to have some influence.

In the course of his lectures on the Three Principles, *San Min Chu I*, Sun had said:

> If we want China to rise to power, we must not only restore our national standing, but we must also assume a great responsibility towards the world. If China cannot assume that great responsibility, she will be a great disadvantage, not an advantage to the world, no matter how strong she may be. What really is our duty to the world? The road which the great powers are travelling today means the destruction of other states. If China, when she becomes strong, wants to crush other countries, copy the Powers' imperialism, and go their road, we will just be following in their tracks. Let us first of all decide on our policy. Only if we rescue the weak and lift up the fallen will we be carrying out the divine obligations of our nation. We must aid the weaker and smaller peoples and oppose the great powers of the world. If all the people of the country

resolve upon this purpose, our nation will prosper; otherwise, there is no hope for us.[3]

Since Sun died the road taken by Japan, Italy, Germany and the United States has come very near its ultimate destination. The rape of Nanking, 'pacification', Auschwitz and the massacre at Song My only dramatize vividly what the beneficiaries of the old social order have been doing to its victims. For Sun it was a prophetic and political task to save mankind from the spiritual and material annihilation promised by that order. He was a modest and humble man, and did not see himself as a messiah. Only in a new material and social order could righteous living be conceivable, and this had to be created by 'the damned of the earth', as Frantz Fanon called them – the coolies of whom Sun was one. In their renunciation of selfish nationalism, of super-power status, and of expansionism and aggression characteristic of the 'developed' nations, in their efforts to build with others what Chairman Mao has termed 'a world belonging to the people', that quarter of mankind living in China has begun building the kind of world in the creation of which Sun was a pioneer. The sanctity of the capitalist system (with its slavish doctrines for the oppressed), of racial privilege, or of the powerful was no part of Sun's Christian creed. Perhaps that explains why righteousness, justice, and personal freedom and dignity are palpable realities in the social order he pioneered.

NOTES

1. Martin, op. cit., p. 226.
2. Quoted in Martin, p. 65.
3. Quoted in C. R. Hensman, *From Gandhi to Guevara*, Allen Lane The Penguin Press 1970, pp. 275–6.